T
Genesis

_____

Presented to

_____

Presented by

_____

Date

_____

Occasion

The Book of Genesis

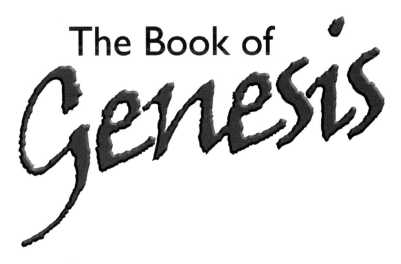

 The Illustrated
International Children's Bible®

Design and Illustration from
Neely Publishing LLC.

Individual contributors:
Keith R. Neely, David Miles, Jim Balkovek, Kevin Davidson,
Roberta Neely, Bridget Harlow and Thomas R. Zuber

THOMAS NELSON, INC.
Since 1798

For other products and live events, visit us at:
www.thomasnelson.com

Introduction

Welcome! You've just picked up one of the most amazing books of all time, the Holy Bible. This book of the Bible, Genesis, is presented in a way that has never been done before. Want to know how and why we've done it this way? Keep reading to find out!

Our Purpose
We did not want to create just another children's Bible story-book. In other words, we didn't want to have Bible pictures alongside words that are a retelling of God's Word, the Holy Scriptures. We wanted to draw attention to, magnify, and clarify the actual Word of God. In those words lies the power to change the lives of children and adults alike!

"God's word is alive and working." Hebrews 4:12

"But the word of the Lord will live forever." 1 Peter 1:25

In the same way that written illustrations or "word pictures" are used to help make an idea easy to understand and memorable, our visual illustrations will make the actual Word of God easier to understand than ever before.

The Illustrated International Children's Bible®
The International Children's Bible® was the first translation created especially for children. It has been illustrated in a frame-by-frame format style. These realistic images help illustrate the actual Scriptures . . . the events of the Bible. The format helps to carry the reader easily through each story like a visual movie. This not only makes the verses easier to understand, but also easier to memorize!

Actual Scriptures:

Yes, that's right . . . the pages of this book are actual Bible verses. On some pages you'll see the characters speaking by the use of a dialog box. The action and setting of the scene is readily apparent by the backgrounds. What a great way to read and learn your Bible! Some of the verses are not a person speaking, so they will be in plain boxes. You might see some small "d's" in the text. These indicate a word that will have a definition in the dictionary found at the back of full ICB Bibles.

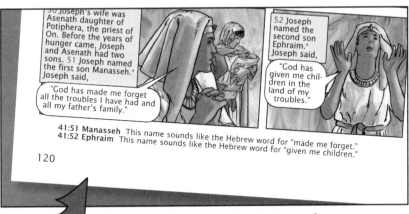

Footnotes appear at the bottom of some pages. They are represented in the Bible verses by a small "n." That will let you know that there is a note at the bottom of the page that gives you a little more information about that word or phrase. Just more information that's helpful to know!

In some chapters and verses there will not be a lot of inter-action between Bible characters, but you will see background scenery, maps, and other interesting treatments to help make your Bible reading more fun and helpful. Most Bible storybooks are just that . . . stories retold to make them easier to under-stand. Never before has actual Bible Scripture been illustrated in this form so that children and adults can immediately read and know what is going on in a certain verse—who was talking, what time of day it was, was it inside or out, who was there. We hope you enjoy reading this Bible and have fun learning along the way!

The Publishers

Look for these other titles.

Coming Soon!

Table of Contents

Chapter 1
The Beginning of the World.............1

Chapter 2
The Seventh Day—Rest..................5
The First People..........................5
The First Woman.........................6

Chapter 3
The Beginning of Sin......................6

Chapter 4
The First Family..........................8
Cain's Family.............................10
Adam and Eve Have a New Son......11

Chapter 5
Adam's Family History................11

Chapter 6
The Human Race Becomes Evil......12
Noah and the Great Flood.............12

Chapter 7
The Flood Begins........................13

Chapter 8
The Flood Ends...........................16

Chapter 9
The New Beginning......................18
Noah and His Sons......................19

Chapter 10
Nations Grow and Spread.............20
Japheth's Sons...........................20
Ham's Sons...............................20
Shem's Sons..............................21

Chapter 11
The Languages Confused.............22
The Story of Shem's Family..........23
The Story of Terah's Family..........23

Chapter 12
God Calls Abram........................24

Abram Goes to Egypt..................25

Chapter 13
Abram and Lot Separate..............26

Chapter 14
Lot Is Captured..........................28
Abram Rescues Lot.....................29

Chapter 15
God's Agreement with Abram.......30

Chapter 16
Hagar and Ishmael......................32

Chapter 17
Proof of the Agreement...............33
Isaac—the Promised Son.............35

Chapter 18
The Three Visitors.......................36
Abraham's Bargain with God........38

Chapter 19
Lot's Visitors.............................39
Sodom and Gomorrah Destroyed..42
Lot and His Daughters.................43

Chapter 20
Abraham and Abimelech..............44

Chapter 21
A Baby for Sarah........................46
Hagar and Ishmael......................47
Abraham's Bargain
with Abimelech 48

Chapter 22
God Tests Abraham....................49

Chapter 23
Sarah Dies................................52

Chapter 24
A Wife for Isaac.........................54

Chapter 25
Abraham's Family.......................62

Isaac's Family..............63

Chapter 26
Isaac Lies to Abimelech............65
Isaac Becomes Rich...........66

Chapter 27
Jacob Tricks Isaac.................68

Chapter 28
Jacob Searches for a Wife...........74
Jacob's Dream at Bethel............75

Chapter 29
Jacob Arrives in Northwest
Mesopotamia.................76
Jacob Is Tricked..................78
Jacob's Family Grows...............79

Chapter 30
Jacob Tricks Laban.................82

Chapter 31
Jacob Runs Away..............84
The Search for the Stolen Idols......85
Jacob and Laban's Agreement.......87

Chapter 32
Jacob Meets Esau..............88
Jacob Wrestles with God............90

Chapter 33
Jacob Shows His Bravery............91

Chapter 34
Dinah Is Attacked.................94

Chapter 35
Jacob in Bethel................97
Jacob's New Name.................98
Rachel Dies Giving Birth............98
The Family of Israel................99

Chapter 36
Esau's Family..............99

Chapter 37
Joseph the Dreamer...............101
Joseph Sold into Slavery..........103

Chapter 38
Judah and Tamar..............105

Chapter 39
Joseph Is Sold to Potiphar.........109
Joseph Is Put into Prison..........109

Chapter 40
Joseph Interprets Two Dreams....112

Chapter 41
The King's Dreams................115
Joseph Tells
the Dreams' Meaning...............118
Joseph Is Made Ruler over Egypt..119

Chapter 42
The Dreams Come True.............122
The Brothers Return to Jacob......125

Chapter 43
The Brothers Go Back to Egypt....126

Chapter 44
Joseph Sets a Trap................131

Chapter 45
Joseph Reveals Who He Is...........134

Chapter 46
Jacob Goes to Egypt...............137
Jacob's Family................138
Jacob Arrives in Egypt.............139

Chapter 47
Jacob Settles in Goshen............140
Joseph Buys Land for the King.....141
"Don't Bury Me in Egypt".........143

Chapter 48
Blessings for Manasseh
and Ephraim.................143

Chapter 49
Jacob Blesses His Sons.............146

Chapter 50
Jacob's Burial................149
The Brother's Fear Joseph..........151
The Death of Joseph................152

Genesis

Chapter

1

The Beginning of the World

1 In the beginning God created the sky and the earth. 2 The earth was empty and had no form. Darkness covered the ocean, and God's Spirit d was moving over the water.

Genesis 1:3-13

3 Then God said,

"Let there be light!"

And there was light.

4 God saw that the light was good. So he divided the light from the darkness.

5 God named the light "day" and the darkness "night." Evening passed, and morning came. This was the first day.

Day 1

6 Then God said,

"Let there be something to divide the water in two!"

7 So God made the air to divide the water in two. Some of the water was above the air, and some of the water was below it. 8 God named the air "sky." Evening passed, and morning came. This was the second day.

Day 2

9 Then God said,

"Let the water under the sky be gathered together so the dry land will appear."

And it happened. 10 God named the dry land "earth." He named the water that was gathered together "seas." God saw that this was good.

11 Then God said,

"Let the earth produce plants. Some plants will make grain for seeds. Others will make fruit with seeds in it. Every seed will produce more of its own kind of plant."

And it happened.

12 The earth produced plants. Some plants had grain for seeds. The trees made fruit with seeds in it. Each seed grew its own kind of plant. God saw that all this was good. 13 Evening passed, and morning came. This was the third day.

Day 3

14 Then God said,

"Let there be lights in the sky to separate day from night. These lights will be used for signs, seasons, days and years. 15 They will be in the sky to give light to the earth."

And it happened. 16 So God made the two large lights. He made the brighter light to rule the day. He made the smaller light to rule the night. He also made the stars. 17 God put all these in the sky to shine on the earth. 18 They are to rule over the day and over the night. He put them there to separate the light from the darkness. God saw that all these things were good. 19 Evening passed, and morning came. This was the fourth day.

Day 4

20 Then God said,

"Let the water be filled with living things. And let birds fly in the air above the earth."

21 So God created the large sea animals. He created every living thing that moves in the sea. The sea is filled with these living things. Each one produces more of its own kind. God also made every bird that flies. And each bird produces more of its own kind. God saw that this was good. 22 God blessed them and said,

"Have many young ones and grow in number. Fill the water of the seas, and let the birds grow in number on the earth."

23 Evening passed, and morning came. This was the fifth day.

Day 5

Genesis 1:24-31

24 Then God said,

"Let the earth be filled with animals. And let each produce more of its own kind. Let there be tame animals and small crawling animals and wild animals. And let each produce more of its kind."

And it happened. 25 So God made the wild animals, the tame animals and all the small crawling animals to produce more of their own kind. God saw that this was good.
26 Then God said,

"Let us make human beings in our image and likeness. And let them rule over the fish in the sea and the birds in the sky. Let them rule over the tame animals, over all the earth and over all the small crawling animals on the earth."

27 So God created human beings in his image. In the image of God he created them. He created them male and female. 28 God blessed them and said,

"Have many children and grow in number. Fill the earth and be its master. Rule over the fish in the sea and over the birds in the sky. Rule over every living thing that moves on the earth."

Day 6

29 God said,

"Look, I have given you all the plants that have grain for seeds. And I have given you all the trees whose fruits have seeds in them. They will be food for you. 30 I have given all the green plants to all the animals to eat. They will be food for every wild animal, every bird of the air and every small crawling animal."

And it happened. 31 God looked at everything he had made, and it was very good. Evening passed, and morning came. This was the sixth day.

Chapter 2

The Seventh Day—Rest

1 So the sky, the earth and all that filled them were finished. 2 By the seventh day God finished the work he had been doing. So on the seventh day he rested from all his work. 3 God blessed the seventh day and made it a holy day. He made it holy because on that day he rested. He rested from all the work he had done in creating the world.

The First People

4 This is the story of the creation of the sky and the earth. When the Lord God made the earth and the sky, 5 there were no plants on the earth. Nothing was growing in the fields. The Lord God had not yet made it rain on the land. And there was no man to care for the ground. 6 But a mist often rose from the earth and watered all the ground.

7 Then the Lord God took dust from the ground and formed man from it. The Lord breathed the breath of life into the man's nose. And the man became a living person.

8 Then the Lord God planted a garden in the East, in a place called Eden. He put the man he had formed in that garden. 9 The Lord God caused every beautiful tree and every tree that was good for food to grow out of the ground. In the middle of the garden, God put the tree that gives life. And he put there the tree that gives the knowledge of good and evil.
10 A river flowed through Eden and watered the garden. From that point the river was divided. It had four streams flowing into it. 11 The name of the first stream is Pishon. It flows around the whole land of Havilah, where there is gold. 12 That gold is good. Bdellium and onyx[n] are also there. 13 The name of the second river is Gihon. It flows around the whole land of Cush. 14 The name of the third river is Tigris. It flows out of Assyria toward the east. The fourth river is the Euphrates.
15 The Lord God put the man in the garden of Eden to care for it and work it. 16 The Lord God commanded him,

"You may eat the fruit from any tree in the garden. 17 But you must not eat the fruit from the tree which gives the knowledge of good and evil. If you ever eat fruit from that tree, you will die!"

2:12 bdellium and onyx Bdellium is an expensive, sweet-smelling resin like myrrh. And onyx is a gem.

Genesis 2:18–3:3

The First Woman

18 Then the Lord God said,

"It is not good for the man to be alone. I will make a helper who is right for him."

19 From the ground God formed every wild animal and every bird in the sky. He brought them to the man so the man could name them. Whatever the man called each living thing, that became its name.

20 The man gave names to all the tame animals, to the birds in the sky and to all the wild animals. But Adam[n] did not find a helper that was right for him.

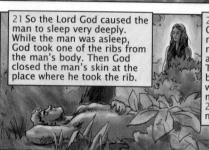

21 So the Lord God caused the man to sleep very deeply. While the man was asleep, God took one of the ribs from the man's body. Then God closed the man's skin at the place where he took the rib.

22 The Lord God used the rib from the man to make a woman. Then the Lord brought the woman to the man. 23 And the man said,

"Now, this is someone whose bones came from my bones. Her body came from my body. I will call her 'woman,' because she was taken out of man."

24 So a man will leave his father and mother and be united with his wife. And the two people will become one body.

25 The man and his wife were naked, but they were not ashamed.

Chapter

3

The Beginning of Sin

1 Now the snake was the most clever of all the wild animals the Lord God had made. One day the snake spoke to the woman. He said,

"Did God really say that you must not eat fruit from any tree in the garden?"

2 The woman answered the snake,

"We may eat fruit from the trees in the garden. 3 But God told us, 'You must not eat fruit from the tree that is in the middle of the garden. You must not even touch it, or you will die.' "

2:20 Adam This is the name of the first man. It also means "humans," including men and women.

4 But the snake said to the woman,

"You will not die. 5 God knows that if you eat the fruit from that tree, you will learn about good and evil. Then you will be like God!"

6 The woman saw that the tree was beautiful. She saw that its fruit was good to eat and that it would make her wise. So she took some of its fruit and ate it. She also gave some of the fruit to her husband who was with her,

and he ate it.

7 Then, it was as if the man's and the woman's eyes were opened. They realized they were naked.

So they sewed fig leaves together and made something to cover themselves. 8 Then they heard the Lord God walking in the garden. This was during the cool part of the day. And the man and his wife hid from the Lord God among the trees in the garden. 9 But the Lord God called to the man. The Lord said,

"Where are you?"

10 The man answered,

"I heard you walking in the garden. I was afraid because I was naked. So I hid."

11 God said to the man,

"Who told you that you were naked? Did you eat fruit from that tree? I commanded you not to eat from that tree."

12 The man said,

"You gave this woman to me. She gave me fruit from the tree. So I ate it."

13 Then the Lord God said to the woman,

"What have you done?"

She answered,

"The snake tricked me. So I ate the fruit."

14 The Lord God said to the snake,

"Because you did this, a curse will be put on you. You will be cursed more than any tame animal or wild animal. You will crawl on your stomach, and you will eat dust all the days of your life. 15 I will make you and the woman enemies to each other. Your descendants[d] and her descendants will be enemies. Her child will crush your head. And you will bite his heel."

16 Then God said to the woman,

"I will cause you to have much trouble when you are pregnant. And when you give birth to children, you will have great pain. You will greatly desire your husband, but he will rule over you."

7

17 Then God said to the man,

"You listened to what your wife said. And you ate fruit from the tree that I commanded you not to eat from.
"So I will put a curse on the ground. You will have to work very hard for food. In pain you will eat its food all the days of your life. 18 The ground will produce thorns and weeds for you. And you will eat the plants of the field. 19 You will sweat and work hard for your food. Later you will return to the ground. This is because you were taken from the ground. You are dust. And when you die, you will return to the dust."

20 The man named his wife Eve.ⁿ This is because she is the mother of everyone who ever lived.
21 The Lord God made clothes from animal skins for the man and his wife. And so the Lord dressed them.

22 Then the Lord God said,

"Look, the man has become like one of us. He knows good and evil. And now we must keep him from eating some of the fruit from the tree of life. If he does, he will live forever."

23 So the Lord God forced the man out of the garden of Eden. He had to work the ground he was taken from. 24 God forced the man out of the garden. Then God put angels on the east side of the garden. He also put a sword of fire there. It flashed around in every direction. This kept people from getting to the tree of life.

Chapter 4

The First Family

1 Adam had sexual relations with his wife Eve. She became pregnant and gave birth to Cain.ⁿ Eve said,

"With the Lord's help, I have given birth to a man."

2 After that, Eve gave birth to Cain's brother Abel. Abel took care of sheep. Cain became a farmer.

3:20 Eve This name sounds like the Hebrew word meaning "alive."
4:1 Cain This name sounds like the Hebrew word for "I have given birth."

3 Later, Cain brought a gift to God. He brought some food from the ground. 4 Abel brought the best parts of his best sheep. The Lord accepted Abel and his gift. 5 But God did not accept Cain and his gift. Cain became very angry and looked unhappy.

6 The Lord asked Cain,

"Why are you angry? Why do you look so unhappy? 7 If you do good, I will accept you. But if you do not do good, sin is ready to attack you. Sin wants you. But you must rule over it."

8 Cain said to his brother Abel,

"Let's go out into the field."

So Cain and Abel went into the field. Then Cain attacked his brother Abel and killed him.

9 Later, the Lord said to Cain,

"Where is your brother Abel?"

Cain answered,

"I don't know. Is it my job to take care of my brother?"

10 Then the Lord said,

"What have you done? Your brother's blood is on the ground. That blood is like a voice that tells me what happened.

Genesis 4:11-22

11 "And now you will be cursed in your work with the ground. It is the same ground where your brother's blood fell. Your hands killed him. 12 You will work the ground. But it will not grow good crops for you anymore. You will wander around on the earth."

13 Then Cain said to the Lord,

"This punishment is more than I can stand!"

14 Look! You have forced me to stop working the ground. And now I must hide from you. I will wander around on the earth. And anyone who meets me can kill me."

15 Then the Lord said to Cain,

"No! If anyone kills you, I will punish that person seven times more."

Then the Lord put a mark on Cain. It was a warning to anyone who met him not to kill him.

Cain's Family

16 Then Cain went away from the Lord. Cain lived in the land of Nod," east of Eden.

17 Cain had sexual relations with his wife. She became pregnant and gave birth to Enoch. At that time Cain was building a city. He named it after his son Enoch.

18 Enoch had a son named Irad. Irad had a son named Mehujael. Mehujael had a son named Methushael. And Methushael had a son named Lamech. 19 Lamech married two women. One wife was named Adah, and the other was Zillah. 20 Adah gave birth to Jabal. He was the first person to live in tents and raise cattle. 21 Jabal's brother was Jubal. Jubal was the first person to play the harp and flute. 22 Zillah gave birth to Tubal-Cain. He made tools out of bronze and iron. The sister of Tubal-Cain was Naamah.

4:16 Nod This name sounds like the Hebrew word for "wander."

23 Lamech said to his wives:

"Adah and Zillah, hear my voice! You wives of Lamech, listen to what I say. I killed a man for wounding me. I killed a young man for hitting me. 24 Cain's killer may be punished 7 times. Then Lamech's killer will be punished 77 times."

Adam and Eve Have a New Son

25 Adam had sexual relations with his wife Eve again. And she gave birth to a son. She named him Seth.ⁿ Eve said,

"God has given me another child. He will take the place of Abel, who was killed by Cain."

26 Seth also had a son. They named him Enosh. At that time people began to pray to the Lord.

Chapter 5

Adam's Family History

1 This is the family history of Adam. When God created human beings, he made them in God's likeness. 2 He created them male and female. And on that day he blessed them and named them human beings. 3 When Adam was 130 years old, he became the father of another son. He was in the likeness and image of Adam. Adam named him Seth. 4 After Seth was born, Adam lived 800 years. During that time he had other sons and daughters. 5 So Adam lived a total of 930 years. Then he died. 6 When Seth was 105 years old, he had a son named Enosh. 7 After Enosh was born, Seth lived 807 years. During that time he had other sons and daughters. 8 So Seth lived a total of 912 years. Then he died. 9 When Enosh was 90 years old, he had a son named Kenan. 10 After Kenan was born, Enosh lived 815 years. During that time he had other sons and daughters. 11 So Enosh lived a total of 905 years. Then he died.

12 When Kenan was 70 years old, he had a son named Mahalalel. 13 After Mahalalel was born, Kenan lived 840 years. During that time he had other sons and daughters. 14 So Kenan lived a total of 910 years. Then he died. 15 When Mahalalel was 65 years old, he had a son named Jared. 16 After Jared was born, Mahalalel lived 830 years. During that time he had other sons and daughters. 17 So Mahalalel lived a total of 895 years. Then he died. 18 When Jared was 162 years old, he had a son named Enoch. 19 After Enoch was born, Jared lived 800 years. During that time he had other sons and daughters. 20 So Jared lived a total of 962 years. Then he died. 21 When Enoch was 65 years old, he had a son named Methuselah. 22 After Methuselah was born, Enoch walked with God 300 years more. During that time he had other sons and daughters. 23 So Enoch lived a total of 365 years. 24 Enoch walked with God. One day Enoch could not be found, because God took him. 25 When Methuselah was 187 years old, he had a son named Lamech. 26 After Lamech was born, Methuselah lived 782 years. During that time he had other sons and daughters. 27 So Methuselah lived a total of 969 years. Then he died. 28 When Lamech was 182, he had a son. 29 Lamech named his son Noah.ⁿ Lamech said,

"Noah will comfort us from the pain of our work. The pain is because God has cursed the ground."

30 After Noah was born, Lamech lived 595 years. During that time he had other sons and daughters. 31 So Lamech lived a total of 777 years. Then he died. 32 After Noah was 500 years old, he became the father of Shem, Ham and Japheth.

4:25 **Seth** This name sounds like the Hebrew word for "to give."
5:29 **Noah** This name sounds like the Hebrew word for "rest."

Chapter 6

The Human Race Becomes Evil

1 The number of people on earth began to grow. Daughters were born to these people. 2 The sons of God saw that these girls were beautiful. And they married any of them they chose. 3 The Lord said,

"My Spirit[d] will not remain in human beings forever. This is because they are flesh. They will live only 120 years."

4 The Nephilim[d] were on the earth in those days and also later. That was when the sons of God had sexual relations with the daughters of men. These women gave birth to children, who became famous. They were the mighty warriors of long ago. 5 The Lord saw that the human beings on the earth were very wicked. He also saw that their thoughts were only about evil all the time. 6 The Lord was sorry he had made human beings on the earth. His heart was filled with pain.

7 So the Lord said,

"I will destroy all human beings that I made on the earth. And I will destroy every animal and everything that crawls on the earth. I will also destroy the birds of the air. This is because I am sorry that I have made them."

8 But Noah pleased the Lord.

Noah and the Great Flood

9 This is the family history of Noah. Noah was a good man. He was the most innocent man of his time. He walked with God. 10 Noah had three sons: Shem, Ham and Japheth. 11 People on earth did what God said was evil. Violence was everywhere. 12 And God saw this evil. All people on the earth did only evil. 13 So God said to Noah,

"People have made the earth full of violence. So I will destroy all people from the earth. 14 Build a boat of cypress wood for yourself.

Make rooms in it and cover it inside and outside with tar. 15 This is how big I want you to build the boat: 450 feet long, 75 feet wide and 45 feet high. 16 Make an opening around the top of the boat. Make it 18 inches high from the edge of the roof down. Put a door in the side of the boat. Make an upper, middle and lower deck in it. 17 I will bring a flood of water on the earth. I will destroy all living things that live under the sky. This includes everything that has the breath of life. Everything on the earth will die. 18 But I will make an agreement with you. You, your sons, your wife and your sons' wives will all go into the boat. 19 Also, you must bring into the boat two of every living thing, male and female. Keep them alive with you. 20 There will be two of every kind of bird, animal and crawling thing. They will come to you to be kept alive. 21 Also gather some of every kind of food. Store it on the boat as food for you and the animals."

22 Noah did everything that God commanded him.

chapter 7

The Flood Begins

1 Then the Lord said to Noah,

"I have seen that you are the best man among the people of this time. So you and your family go into the boat. 2 Take with you seven pairs, each male with its female, of every kind of clean[d] animal. And take one pair, each male with its female, of every kind of unclean animal. 3 Take seven pairs of all the birds of the sky, each male with its female. This will allow all these animals to continue living on the earth after the flood. 4 Seven days from now I will send rain on the earth. It will rain 40 days and 40 nights. I will destroy from the earth every living thing that I made."

5 Noah did everything that the Lord commanded him.

6 Noah was 600 years old when the flood came. 7 He and his wife and his sons and their wives went into the boat. They went in to escape the waters of the flood. 8 The clean animals, the unclean animals, the birds and everything that crawls on the ground 9 came to Noah. They went into the boat in groups of two, male and female. This was just as God had commanded Noah. 10 Seven days later the flood started.

11 Noah was now 600 years old. The flood started on the seventeenth day of the second month of that year. That day the underground springs split open. And the clouds in the sky poured out rain. 12 The rain fell on the earth for 40 days and 40 nights.
13 On that same day Noah and his wife, his sons Shem, Ham and Japheth and their wives went into the boat. 14 They

had every kind of wild animal and tame animal. There was every kind of animal that crawls on the earth. Every kind of bird was there. 15 They all came to Noah in the boat in groups of two. There was every creature that had the breath of life. 16 One male and one female of every living thing came. It was just as God had commanded Noah. Then the Lord closed the door behind them.

17 Water flooded the earth for 40 days. As the water rose, it lifted the boat off the ground. 18 The water continued to rise, and the boat floated on the water above the earth. 19 The water rose so much that even the highest mountains under the sky were covered by it. 20 The water continued to rise until it was more than 20 feet above the mountains. 21 All living things that moved on the earth died. This included all the birds, tame animals, wild animals and creatures that swarm on the earth. And all human beings died. 22 So everything on dry land died. This means everything that had the breath of life in its nose. 23 So God destroyed from the earth every living thing that was on the land. This was every man, animal, crawling thing and bird of the sky. All that was left was Noah and what was with him in the boat. 24 And the waters continued to cover the earth for 150 days.

Chapter 8

The Flood Ends

1 But God remembered Noah and all the wild animals and tame animals with him in the boat. God made a wind blow over the earth. And the water went down. 2 The underground springs stopped flowing. And the clouds in the sky stopped pouring down rain. 3-4 The water that covered the earth began to go down. After 150 days the water had gone down so much that the boat touched land again. It came to rest on one of the mountains of Ararat.[n] This was on the seventeenth day of the seventh month.

5 The water continued to go down. By the first day of the tenth month the tops of the mountains could be seen.
6 Forty days later Noah opened the window he had made in the boat. 7 He sent out a raven. It flew here and there until the water had dried up from the earth.

8 Then Noah sent out a dove. This was to find out if the water had dried up from the ground. 9 The dove could not find a place to land because water still covered the earth. So it came back to the boat. Noah reached out his hand and took the bird. And he brought it back into the boat.

10 After seven days Noah again sent out the dove from the boat. 11 And that evening it came back to him with a fresh olive leaf in its mouth.

Then Noah knew that the ground was almost dry. 12 Seven days later he sent the dove out again. But this time it did not come back.

8:3-4 **Ararat** The ancient land of Urartu, an area in Eastern Turkey.

13 Noah was now 601 years old. It was the first day of the first month of that year. The water was dried up from the land. Noah removed the covering of the boat and saw that the land was dry. 14 By the twenty-seventh day of the second month the land was completely dry.
15 Then God said to Noah,

16 "You and your wife, your sons and their wives should go out of the boat.
17 Bring every animal out of the boat with you—the birds, animals and everything that crawls on the earth. Let them have many young ones and let them grow in number."

18 So Noah went out with his sons, his wife and his sons' wives. 19 Every animal, everything that crawls on the earth and every bird went out of the boat. They left by families.
20 Then Noah built an altar to the Lord. Noah took some of all the clean[d] birds and animals. And he burned them on the altar as offerings to God. 21 The Lord was pleased with these sacrifices. He said to himself,

"I will never again curse the ground because of human beings. Their thoughts are evil even when they are young. But I will never again destroy every living thing on the earth as I did this time.
22 "As long as the earth continues, there will be planting and harvest. Cold and hot, summer and winter, day and night will not stop."

Chapter 9

The New Beginning

1 Then God blessed Noah and his sons. He said to them,

"Have many children. Grow in number and fill the earth. 2 Every animal on earth and every bird in the sky will respect and fear you. So will every animal that crawls on the ground and every fish in the sea respect and fear you. I have given them to you. 3 "Everything that moves, everything that is alive, is yours for food. Earlier I gave you the green plants. And now I give you everything for food. 4 But you must not eat meat that still has blood in it, because blood gives life. 5 I will demand your blood for your lives. That is, I will demand the life of any animal that kills a person. And I will demand the life of anyone who takes another person's life. 6 "Whoever kills a human being will be killed by a human being. This is because God made humans in his own image. 7 "Noah, I want you and your family to have many children. Grow in number on the earth and become many."

8 Then God said to Noah and his sons,

9 "Now I am making my agreement with you and your people who will live after you. 10 And I also make it with every living thing that is with you. It is with the birds, the tame animals and the wild animals. It is with all that came out of the boat with you. I make my agreement with every living thing on earth.

11 I make this agreement with you: I will never again destroy all living things by floodwaters. A flood will never again destroy the earth."

12 And God said,

"I am making an agreement between me and you and every living creature that is with you. It will continue from now on. This is the sign: 13 I am putting my rainbow in the clouds. It is the sign of the agreement between me and the earth. 14 When I bring clouds over the earth, a rainbow appears in the clouds. 15 Then I will remember my agreement. It is between me and you and every living thing. Floodwaters will never again destroy all life on the earth. 16 When the rainbow appears in the clouds, I will see it. Then I will remember the agreement that continues forever. It is between me and every living thing on the earth."

17 So God said to Noah,

"That rainbow is a sign. It is the sign of the agreement that I made with all living things on earth."

Noah and His Sons

18 The sons of Noah came out of the boat with him. They were Shem, Ham and Japheth. (Ham was the father of Canaan.) 19 These three men were Noah's sons. And all the people on earth came from these three sons.

20 Noah became a farmer and planted a vineyard.

21 He drank wine made from his grapes. Then he became drunk and lay naked in his tent. 22 Ham, the father of Canaan, looked at his naked father. Ham told his brothers outside. 23 Then Shem and Japheth got a coat and carried it on both their shoulders. They walked backwards into the tent and covered their father. They turned their faces away. In this way they did not see their father without clothes. 24 Noah was sleeping because of the wine. Later he woke up. Then he learned what his youngest son, Ham, had done to him.

25 So Noah said,

"May there be a curse on Canaan! May he be the lowest slave to his brothers."

26 Noah also said,

"May the Lord, the God of Shem, be praised! May Canaan be Shem's slave. 27 May God give more land to Japheth. May Japheth live in Shem's tents, and may Canaan be their slave."

28 After the flood Noah lived 350 years. 29 He lived a total of 950 years. Then he died.

19

Chapter

10

Nations Grow and Spread

1 This is the family history of the sons of Noah: Shem, Ham and Japheth. After the flood these three men had sons.

Japheth's Sons

2 The sons of Japheth were Gomer, Magog, Madai, Javan, Tubal, Meshech and Tiras.
3 The sons of Gomer were Ashkenaz, Riphath and Togarmah.
4 The sons of Javan were Elishah, Tarshish, Kittim[n] and Rodanim.
5 Those who lived in the lands around the Mediterranean Sea came from these sons of Japheth. All the families grew and became different nations. Each nation had its own land and its own language.

Ham's Sons

6 The sons of Ham were Cush, Mizraim,[n] Put and Canaan.
7 The sons of Cush were Seba, Havilah, Sabtah, Raamah and Sabteca.
The sons of Raamah were Sheba and Dedan.
8 Cush also had a descendant[d] named Nimrod. Nimrod became a very powerful man on earth. 9 He was a great hunter before the Lord. That is why people say someone is "like Nimrod, a great hunter before the Lord." 10 At first Nimrod's kingdom covered Babylon, Erech, Akkad and Calneh in the land of Babylonia. 11 From there he went to Assyria. There he built the cities of Nineveh, Rehoboth Ir and Calah. 12 He also built Resen, the great city between Nineveh and Calah.
13 Mizraim was the father of the Ludites, Anamites, Lehabites, Naphtuhites, 14 Pathrusites, Casluhites and the people of Crete. (The Philistines came from the Casluhites.)
15 Canaan was the father of Sidon his first son and of Heth.

10:4 **Kittim** His descendants were the people of Cyprus.
10:6 **Mizraim** This is another name for Egypt.

16 Canaan was also the father of the Jebusites, Amorites, Girgashites, 17 Hivites, Arkites, Sinites, 18 Arvadites, Zemarites and Hamathites. The families of the Canaanites scattered. 19 The land of the Canaanites reached from Sidon to Gerar as far as Gaza. And it reached to Sodom, Gomorrah, Admah and Zeboiim, as far as Lasha. 20 All these people were the sons of Ham. All these families had their own languages, their own lands and their own nations.

Shem's Sons

21 Shem, Japheth's older brother, also had sons. One of his descendants[d] was the father of all the sons of Eber. 22 The sons of Shem were Elam, Asshur, Arphaxad, Lud and Aram. 23 The sons of Aram were Uz, Hul, Gether and Meshech. 24 Arphaxad was the father of Shelah. Shelah was the father of Eber. 25 Eber was the father of two sons. One son was named Peleg[n] because the earth was divided during his life. Eber's other son was named Joktan. 26 Joktan was the father of Almodad, Sheleph, Hazarmaveth, Jerah, 27 Hadoram, Uzal, Diklah, 28 Obal, Abimael, Sheba, 29 Ophir, Havilah and Jobab. All these people were the sons of Joktan. 30 These people lived in the area between Mesha and Sephar in the hill country in the East.

31 These are the people from the family of Shem. They are arranged by families, languages, countries and nations. 32 This is the list of the families from the sons of Noah. They are arranged according to their nations. From these families came all the nations who spread across the earth after the flood.

10:25 Peleg This name sounds like the Hebrew word for "divided."

Chapter 11

The Languages Confused

1 At this time the whole world spoke one language. Everyone used the same words. 2 As people moved from the East, they found a plain in the land of Babylonia. They settled there to live. 3 They said to each other,

"Let's make bricks and bake them to make them hard."

So they used bricks instead of stones, and tar instead of mortar. 4 Then they said to each other,

"Let's build for ourselves a city and a tower. And let's make the top of the tower reach high into the sky. We will become famous. If we do this, we will not be scattered over all the earth."

5 The Lord came down to see the city and the tower that the people had built. 6 The Lord said,

"Now, these people are united. They all speak the same language. This is only the beginning of what they will do. They will be able to do anything they want. 7 Come, let us go down and confuse their language. Then they will not be able to understand each other."

8 So the Lord scattered them from there over all the earth. And they stopped building the city.

9 That is where the Lord confused the language of the whole world. So the place is called Babel." So the Lord caused them to spread out from there over all the whole world.

11:9 Babel This name sounds like the Hebrew word for "confused."

The Story of Shem's Family

10 This is the family history of Shem. Two years after the flood, when Shem was 100 years old, his son Arphaxad was born. 11 After that, Shem lived 500 years and had other sons and daughters.
12 When Arphaxad was 35 years old, his son Shelah was born. 13 After that, Arphaxad lived 403 years and had other sons and daughters.
14 When Shelah was 30 years old, his son Eber was born. 15 After that, Shelah lived 403 years and had other sons and daughters.
16 When Eber was 34 years old, his son Peleg was born. 17 After that, Eber lived 430 years and had other sons and daughters.
18 When Peleg was 30 years old, his son Reu was born.

19 After that, Peleg lived 209 years and had other sons and daughters.
20 When Reu was 32 years old, his son Serug was born. 21 After that, Reu lived 207 years and had other sons and daughters.
22 When Serug was 30 years old, his son Nahor was born. 23 After that, Serug lived 200 years and had other sons and daughters.
24 When Nahor was 29 years old, his son Terah was born. 25 After that, Nahor lived 119 years and had other sons and daughters.
26 After Terah was 70 years old, his sons Abram, Nahor and Haran were born.

The Story of Terah's Family

27 This is the family history of Terah. Terah was the

father of Abram, Nahor and Haran. Haran was the father of Lot. 28 Haran died while his father, Terah, was still alive. This happened in Ur in Babylonia, where he was born. 29 Abram and Nahor both married. Abram's wife was named Sarai. Nahor's wife was named Milcah. She was the daughter of Haran. Haran was the father of Milcah and Iscah. 30 Sarai was not able to have children.
31 Terah took his son Abram, his grandson Lot (Haran's son) and his daughter-in-law Sarai (Abram's wife). They moved out of Ur of Babylonia. They had planned to go to the land of Canaan. But when they reached the city of Haran, they settled there.
32 Terah lived to be 205 years old. Then he died in Haran.

Genesis 12:1-7

Chapter 12

God Calls Abram

1 Then the Lord said to Abram,

"Leave your country, your relatives and your father's family. Go to the land I will show you. 2 I will make you a great nation, and I will bless you. I will make you famous. And you will be a blessing to others. 3 I will bless those who bless you. I will place a curse on those who harm you. And all the people on earth will be blessed through you."

4 So Abram left Haran as the Lord had told him. And Lot went with him. At this time Abram was 75 years old. 5 Abram took his wife Sarai, his nephew Lot and everything they owned. They took all the servants they had gotten in Haran. They set out from Haran, planning to go to the land of Canaan. In time they arrived there. 6 Abram traveled through that land. He went as far as the great tree of Moreh at Shechem. The Canaanites were living in the land at that time.

7 The Lord appeared to Abram. The Lord said,

"I will give this land to your descendants."[d]

So Abram built an altar there to the Lord, who had appeared to him.

8 Then Abram traveled from Shechem to the mountain east of Bethel. And he set up his tent there. Bethel was to the west, and Ai was to the east. There Abram built another altar to the Lord and worshiped him. 9 After this, he traveled on toward southern Canaan.

Abram Goes to Egypt

10 At this time there was not much food in the land. So Abram went down to Egypt to live because there was so little food.

11 Just before they arrived in Egypt, Abram said to his wife Sarai,

"I know you are a very beautiful woman. 12 When the Egyptians see you, they will say, 'This woman is his wife.' Then they will kill me but let you live. 13 Tell them you are my sister. Then things will go well with me. And I may be allowed to live because of you."

14 So Abram went into Egypt. The people of Egypt saw that Sarai was very beautiful.

15 Some of the Egyptian officers saw her also. They told the king of Egypt how beautiful she was. They took her to the king's palace. 16 The king was kind to Abram because he thought Abram was Sarai's brother. He gave Abram sheep, cattle and male and female donkeys. Abram also was given male and female servants and camels.

25

17 But the Lord sent terrible diseases on the king and all the people in his house. This was because of Abram's wife Sarai. 18 So the king sent for Abram. The king said,

"What have you done to me? Why didn't you tell me Sarai was your wife? 19 Why did you say, 'She is my sister'? I made her my wife.

But now here is your wife. Take her and leave!"

20 Then the king commanded his men to make Abram leave Egypt.

So Abram and his wife left with everything they owned.

Chapter 13

Abram and Lot Separate

1 So Abram, his wife and Lot left Egypt. They took everything they owned and traveled to southern Canaan. 2 Abram was very rich in cattle, silver and gold. 3 He left southern Canaan and went back to Bethel. He went where he had camped before, between Bethel and Ai. 4 It was the place where Abram had built an altar before. So he worshiped the Lord there.

5 During this time Lot was traveling with Abram. Lot also had many sheep, cattle and tents. 6 Abram and Lot had so many animals that the land could not support both of them together.

7 Abram's herders and Lot's herders began to argue. The Canaanites and the Perizzites were living in the land at this time. 8 So Abram said to Lot,

"There should be no arguing between you and me. Your herders and mine should not argue either. We are brothers. 9 We should separate. The whole land is there in front of you. If you go to the left, I will go to the right. If you go to the right, I will go to the left."

10 Lot looked all around and saw the whole Jordan Valley. He saw that there was much water there. It was like the Lord's garden, like the land of Egypt in the direction of Zoar. (This was before the Lord destroyed Sodom and Gomorrah.) 11 So Lot chose to move east and live in the Jordan Valley. In this way Abram and Lot separated.

12 Abram lived in the land of Canaan. But Lot lived among the cities in the Jordan Valley. He moved very near to Sodom. 13 Now the people of Sodom were very evil. They were always sinning against the Lord.

Hebron

Dead Sea

Sodom

14 After Lot left, the Lord said to Abram,

"Look all around you. Look north and south and east and west. 15 All this land that you see I will give to you and your descendants[d] forever. 16 I will make your descendants as many as the dust of the earth. If anyone could count the dust on the earth, he could count your people. 17 Get up! Walk through all this land. I am now giving it to you."

18 So Abram moved his tents. He went to live near the great trees of Mamre. This was at the city of Hebron. There he built an altar to the Lord.

Chapter

14

Lot Is Captured

1 Now Amraphel was king of Babylonia. Arioch was king of Ellasar. Kedorlaomer was king of Elam. And Tidal was king of Goiim. 2 All these kings went to war against several other kings: Bera king of Sodom, Birsha king of Gomorrah, Shinab king of Admah, Shemeber king of Zeboiim and the king of Bela. (Bela is also called Zoar.) 3 These kings who were attacked united their armies in the Valley of Siddim. (The Valley of Siddim is now the Dead Sea.ᵈ) 4 These kings had served Kedorlaomer for 12 years. But in the thirteenth year, they all turned against him. 5 Then in the fourteenth year, Kedorlaomer and the kings with him came and defeated the Rephaitesᵈ in Ashteroth Karnaim. They also defeated the Zuzites in Ham and the Emites in Shaveh Kiriathaim. 6 And they defeated the Horites in the mountains of Edom to El Paran. (El Paran is near the desert.) 7 Then they turned back and went to En Mishpat (that is, Kadesh). They defeated all the Amalekites. They also defeated the Amorites who lived in Hazazon Tamar. 8 At that time the kings of Sodom, Gomorrah, Admah, Zeboiim and Bela went out to fight in the Valley of Siddim. (Bela is called Zoar.) 9 They fought against Kedorlaomer king of Elam, Tidal king of Goiim, Amraphel king of Babylonia, and Arioch king of Ellasar. So there were four kings fighting against five. 10 There were many tar pits in the Valley of Siddim. The kings of Sodom and Gomorrah and their armies ran away. Some of the soldiers fell into the tar pits. But the others ran away to the mountains. 11 Now Kedorlaomer and his armies took everything the people of Sodom and Gomorrah owned. They also took all their food. 12 They took Lot, Abram's nephew who was living in Sodom. The enemy also took everything he owned. Then they left.

13 One of the men who was not captured went to Abram, the Hebrew. He told Abram what had happened. At that time Abram was camped near the great trees of Mamre the Amorite. Mamre was a brother of Eshcol and a brother of Aner. And they had all made an agreement to help Abram.

Abram Rescues Lot

14 Abram learned that Lot had been captured. So he called out his 318 trained men who had been born in his camp. Abram led the men and chased the enemy all the way to the town of Dan.

15 That night he divided his men into groups. And they made a surprise attack against the enemy.

They chased them all the way to Hobah, north of Damascus.

16 Then Abram brought back everything the enemy had stolen. Abram brought back the women and the other people. And he also brought back Lot and everything Lot owned.

17 After defeating Kedorlaomer and the kings who were with him, Abram went home. As Abram was returning, the king of Sodom came out to meet him in the Valley of Shaveh. (That is now called King's Valley.)

18 Melchizedek king of Salem also went to meet Abram. Melchizedek was a priest for God Most High. He brought bread and wine. 19 Melchizedek blessed Abram and said,

"Abram, may God Most High give you blessings. God made heaven and earth. 20 And we praise God Most High. He has helped you to defeat your enemies."

Then Abram gave Melchizedek a tenth of everything he had brought back from the battle.

29

Genesis 14:21–15:9

21 Then the king of Sodom said to Abram,

"You may keep all these things for yourself. Just give me my people who were captured."

22 But Abram said to the king of Sodom,

"I make a promise to the Lord. He is the God Most High, who made heaven and earth. 23 I promise that I will not keep anything that is yours. I will not keep even a thread or a sandal strap. That way you cannot say, 'I made Abram rich.' 24 I will keep nothing but the food my young men have eaten. But give Aner, Eshcol and Mamre their share of what we won. They went with me into battle."

Chapter 15

God's Agreement with Abram

1 After these things happened, the Lord spoke his word to Abram in a vision. God said,

"Abram, don't be afraid. I will defend you. And I will give you a great reward."

2 But Abram said,

"Lord God, what can you give me? I have no son. So my slave Eliezer from Damascus will get everything I own after I die."

3 Abram said,

"Look, you have given me no son. So a slave born in my house will inherit everything I have."

4 Then the Lord spoke his word to Abram. He said,

"That slave will not be the one to inherit what you have. You will have a son of your own. And your son will inherit what you have."

5 Then God led Abram outside. God said,

"Look at the sky. There are so many stars you cannot count them. And your descendants[d] will be too many to count."

6 Abram believed the Lord. And the Lord accepted Abram's faith, and that faith made him right with God.

7 God said to Abram,

"I am the Lord who led you out of Ur of Babylonia. I did that so I could give you this land to own."

8 But Abram said,

"Lord God, how can I be sure that I will own this land?"

9 The Lord said to Abram,

"Bring me a three-year-old cow, a three-year-old goat and a three-year-old male sheep. Also bring me a dove and a young pigeon."

10 Abram brought them all to God. Then Abram killed the animals and cut each of them into two pieces. He laid each half opposite the other half. But he did not cut the birds in half. 11 Later, large birds flew down to eat the animals. But Abram chased them away.

12 As the sun was going down, Abram fell into a deep sleep. While he was asleep, a very terrible darkness came. 13 Then the Lord said to Abram,

"You can be sure that your descendants will be strangers and travel in a land they don't own. The people there will make them slaves. And they will do cruel things to them for 400 years. 14 But I will punish the nation where they are slaves. Then your descendants will leave that land, taking great wealth with them. 15 Abram, you will live to be very old. You will die in peace and will be buried. 16 After your great-great-grandchildren are born, your people will come to this land again. It will take that long, because the Amorites are not yet evil enough to punish."

17 The sun went down, and it was very dark. Suddenly a smoking firepot and a blazing torch passed between the halves of the dead animals.ⁿ 18 So on that day the Lord made an agreement with Abram. The Lord said,

"I will give this land to your descendants. I will give them the land between the river of Egypt and the great river Euphrates. 19 This is the land of the Kenites, Kenizzites, Kadmonites, 20 Hittites, Perizzites, Rephaites,ᵈ 21 Amorites, Canaanites, Girgashites and Jebusites."

15:17 passed . . . animals This showed that God sealed the agreement between himself and Abram.

31

Chapter

16

Hagar and Ishmael

1 Sarai, Abram's wife, had no children. She had a slave girl from Egypt named Hagar. 2 Sarai said to Abram,

"Look, the Lord has not allowed me to have children. So have sexual relations with my slave girl. If she has a child, maybe I can have my own family through her."

Abram did what Sarai said. 3 This was after Abram lived ten years in Canaan. And Sarai gave Hagar to her husband Abram. (Hagar was her slave girl from Egypt.)

4 Abram had sexual relations with Hagar, and she became pregnant. When Hagar learned she was pregnant, she began to treat her mistress Sarai badly.

5 Then Sarai said to Abram,

"This is your fault. I gave my slave girl to you. And when she became pregnant, she began to treat me badly. Let the Lord decide who is right—you or me."

6 But Abram said to Sarai,

"You are Hagar's mistress. Do anything you want to her."

Then Sarai was hard on Hagar, and Hagar ran away.

7 The angel of the Lord found Hagar beside a spring of water in the desert. The spring was by the road to Shur. 8 The angel said,

"Hagar, you are Sarai's slave girl. Where have you come from? Where are you going?"

Hagar answered,

"I am running from my mistress Sarai."

9 The angel of the Lord said to her,

"Go home to your mistress and obey her."

10 The angel of the Lord also said,

"I will give you so many descendants[d] they cannot be counted."

11 The angel also said to her,

"You are now pregnant, and you will have a son. You will name him Ishmael,[n] because the Lord has heard your cries. 12 Ishmael will be like a wild donkey. He will be against everyone. And everyone will be against him. He will attack all his brothers."

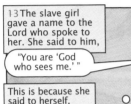

13 The slave girl gave a name to the Lord who spoke to her. She said to him,

"You are 'God who sees me.' "

This is because she said to herself,

"Have I really seen God who sees me?"

14 So the well there was called Beer Lahai Roi.[n] It is between Kadesh and Bered.

15 Hagar gave birth to a son for Abram. And Abram named him Ishmael. 16 Abram was 86 years old when Hagar gave birth to Ishmael.

Chapter

17

Proof of the Agreement

1 When Abram was 99 years old, the Lord appeared to him. The Lord said,

"I am God All-Powerful. Obey me and do what is right.

2 I will make an agreement between us. I will make you the ancestor of many people."

16:11 Ishmael The Hebrew words for "Ishmael" and "has heard" sound similar.
16:14 Beer Lahai Roi This means "the well of the Living One who sees me."

33

3 Then Abram bowed face-down on the ground. God said to him,

4 "I am making my agreement with you: I will make you the father of many nations. 5 I am changing your name from Abram[n] to Abraham.[n] This is because I am making you a father of many nations. 6 I will give you many descendants.[d] New nations will be born from you. Kings will come from you. 7 And I will make an agreement between me and you and all your descendants from now on: I will be your God and the God of all your descendants. 8 You live in the land of Canaan now as a stranger. But I will give you and your descendants all this land forever. And I will be the God of your descendants."

9 Then God said to Abraham,

"You and your descendants must keep this agreement from now on. 10 This is my agreement with you and all your descendants: Every male among you must be circumcised.[d] You must obey this agreement. 11 Cut away the foreskin to show that you follow the agreement between me and you. 12 From now on when a baby boy is eight days old, you will circumcise him. This includes any boy born among your people or any who is your slave. (He would not be one of your descendants.) 13 So circumcise every baby boy. Circumcise him whether he is born in your family or bought as a slave. Your bodies will be marked. This will show that you are part of my agreement that lasts forever. 14 Any male who is not circumcised will be separated from his people. He has broken my agreement."

17:5 **Abram** This name means "honored father."
17:5 **Abraham** The end of the Hebrew word for "Abraham" sounds like the beginning of the Hebrew word for "many."

Isaac—the Promised Son

15 God said to Abraham,

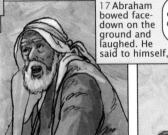

"I will change the name of Sarai,ⁿ your wife. Her new name will be Sarah.ⁿ 16 I will bless her. I will give her a son, and you will be the father. She will be the mother of many nations. Kings of nations will come from her."

17 Abraham bowed face-down on the ground and laughed. He said to himself,

"Can a man have a child when he is 100 years old? Can Sarah give birth to a child when she is 90?"

18 Then Abraham said to God,

"Please let Ishmael be the son you promised."

19 God said,

"No. Sarah your wife will have a son, and you will name him Isaac.ⁿ I will make my agreement with him. It will be an agreement that continues forever with all his descendants.ᵈ 20 "You asked me about Ishmael, and I heard you. I will bless him. I will give him many descendants. And I will cause their numbers to grow very greatly. He will be the father of 12 great leaders. I will make him into a great nation. 21 But I will make my agreement with Isaac. He is the son whom Sarah will have at this same time next year."

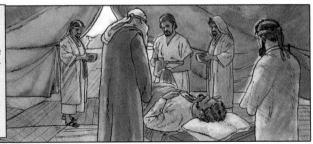

22 After God finished talking with Abraham, God rose and left him. 23 Then Abraham gathered Ishmael and all the males born in his camp. He also gathered the slaves he had bought. So that day Abraham circumcised every man and boy in his camp. This was what God had told him to do.

24 Abraham was 99 years old when he was circumcised. 25 And Ishmael, his son, was 13 years old when he was circumcised. 26 Abraham and his son were circumcised on that same day. 27 Also on that day all the men in Abraham's camp were circumcised. This included all those born in his camp and all the slaves he had bought from other nations.

17:15 **Sarai** An Aramaic name meaning "princess."
17:15 **Sarah** A Hebrew name meaning "princess."
17:19 **Isaac** The Hebrew words for "he laughed" (vs. 17) and "Isaac" sound the same.

Chapter 18

The Three Visitors

1 Later, the Lord again appeared to Abraham near the great trees of Mamre. At that time Abraham was sitting at the door of his tent. It was during the hottest part of the day.

2 He looked up and saw three men standing near him.

When Abraham saw them, he ran from his tent to meet them. He bowed facedown on the ground before them. 3 Abraham said,

"Sir, if you think well of me, please stay awhile with me, your servant. 4 I will bring some water so all of you can wash your feet. You may rest under the tree. 5 I will get some bread for you, so you can regain your strength. Then you may continue your journey."

The three men said,

"That is fine. Do as you said."

6 Abraham hurried to the tent where Sarah was. He said to her,

"Hurry, prepare 20 quarts of fine flour. Make it into loaves of bread."

7 Then Abraham ran to his cattle. He took one of his best calves and gave it to a servant. The servant hurried to kill the calf and to prepare it for food.

8 Abraham gave the three men the calf that had been cooked. He also gave them milk curds and milk. While the three men ate, he stood under the tree near them.

9 The men asked Abraham,

"Where is your wife Sarah?"

"There, in the tent," said Abraham.

10 Then the Lord said,

"I will certainly return to you about this time a year from now. At that time your wife Sarah will have a son."

Sarah was listening at the entrance of the tent which was behind him.

11 Abraham and Sarah were very old. Sarah was past the age when women normally have children. 12 So she laughed to herself,

"My husband and I are too old to have a baby."

13 Then the Lord said to Abraham,

"Why did Sarah laugh? Why did she say, 'I am too old to have a baby'? 14 Is anything too hard for the Lord? No! I will return to you at the right time a year from now. And Sarah will have a son."

15 Sarah was afraid. So she lied and said,

"I didn't laugh."

But the Lord said,

"No. You did laugh."

16 Then the men got up to leave and started out toward Sodom. Abraham walked along with them a short time to send them on their way.

Abraham's Bargain with God

17 The Lord said,

"Should I tell Abraham what I am going to do now? 18 Abraham's children will certainly become a great and powerful nation. And all nations on earth will be blessed through him. 19 I have chosen him so he would command his children and his descendants^d to live the way the Lord wants them to. I did this so they would live right and be fair. Then I, the Lord, will give Abraham what I promised him."

20 Then the Lord said,

"I have heard many things against the people of Sodom and Gomorrah. They are very evil. 21 So I will go down and see if they are as bad as I have heard."

22 So the men turned and went toward Sodom. But Abraham stood there before the Lord. 23 Then Abraham approached the Lord. Abraham asked,

"Lord, do you plan to destroy the good persons along with the evil persons? 24 What if there are 50 good people in that city? Will you still destroy it? Surely you will save the city for the 50 good people living there. 25 Surely you will not destroy the good people along with the evil people. Then the good people and the evil people would be treated the same. You are the judge of all the earth. Won't you do what is right?"

26 Then the Lord said,

"If I find 50 good people in the city of Sodom, I will save the whole city because of them."

27 Then Abraham said,

"I am only dust and ashes. Yet I have been brave to speak to the Lord. 28 What if there are only 45 good people in the city? Will you destroy the whole city for the lack of 5 good people?"

The Lord said,

"If I find 45 good people there, I will not destroy the city."

29 Again Abraham said to the Lord,

"If you find only 40 good people there, will you destroy the city?"

The Lord said,

"If I find 40 good people, I will not destroy the city."

30 Then Abraham said,

"Lord, please don't be angry with me. Let me ask you this. If you find only 30 good people in the city, will you destroy it?"

The Lord said,

"If I find 30 good people there, I will not destroy the city."

31 Then Abraham said,

"I have been brave to speak to the Lord. But what if there are 20 good people in the city?"

The Lord answered,

"If I find 20 good people there, I will not destroy the city."

32 Then Abraham said,

"Lord, please don't be angry with me. Let me bother you this one last time. What if you find 10 good people there?"

The Lord said,

"If I find 10 good people there, I will not destroy it."

33 When the Lord finished speaking to Abraham, he left. And Abraham returned home.

Chapter 19

Lot's Visitors

1 The two angels came to Sodom in the evening. Lot was sitting near the city gate and saw them.

He got up and went to them and bowed facedown on the ground. 2 Lot said,

"Sirs, please come to my house and spend the night. There you can wash your feet. Then tomorrow you may continue your journey."

The angels answered,

"No, we will spend the night in the city's public square."

3 But Lot begged them to come to his house. So they agreed and went to his house. Then Lot prepared a meal for them. He baked bread without yeast, and they ate it.

4 Before bedtime, all the men of the city surrounded Lot's house. These men were both young and old and came from every part of Sodom. 5 They called to Lot,

"Where are the two men who came to you tonight? Bring them out to us. We want to have sexual relations with them."

6 Lot went outside to them, closing the door behind him. 7 He said,

"No, my brothers! Do not do this evil thing. 8 Look! I have two daughters. They have never slept with a man. I will give them to you. You may do anything you want with them. But please don't do anything to these men. They have come to my house, and I must protect them."

9 The men around the house answered,

"Move out of the way!"

Then they said to each other,

"This man Lot came to our city as a stranger. Now he wants to tell us what to do!"

They said to Lot,

"We will do worse things to you than to them."

So they started pushing Lot back. They were ready to break down the door.

11 The two men struck the men outside the door with blindness. So these men, both young and old, could not find the door.

10 But the two men staying with Lot opened the door and pulled him back inside the house. Then they closed the door.

12 The two men said to Lot,

"Do you have any other relatives in this city? Do you have any sons-in-law, sons, daughters or any other relatives? If you do, tell them to leave now. 13 We are about to destroy this city. The Lord has heard of all the evil that is here. So he has sent us to destroy it."

14 So Lot went out and spoke to his future sons-in-law. They were pledged to marry his daughters. Lot said,

"Hurry and leave this city! The Lord is about to destroy it!"

But they thought Lot was joking.

15 At dawn the next morning, the angels begged Lot to hurry. They said,

"Go! Take your wife and your two daughters with you. Then you will not be destroyed when the city is punished."

16 But Lot delayed. So the two men took the hands of Lot, his wife and his two daughters. The men led them safely out of the city. So the Lord was merciful to Lot and his family. 17 The two men brought Lot and his family out of the city. Then one of the men said,

"Run for your lives! Don't look back or stop anywhere in the valley. Run to the mountains or you will be destroyed."

Genesis 19:18-25

18 But Lot said to one of them,

"Sir, please don't force me to go so far! 19 You have been merciful and kind to me. You have saved my life. But I can't run to the mountains. The disaster will catch me, and I will die.

20 Look, that little town over there is not too far away. Let me run there. It's really just a little town. I'll be safe there."

21 The angel said to Lot,

"Very well, I will allow you to do this also. I will not destroy that town. 22 But run there fast. I cannot destroy Sodom until you are safely in that town."

(That town is named Zoar" because it is little.)

Sodom and Gomorrah Destroyed

23 The sun had already come up when Lot entered Zoar.

24 The Lord sent a rain of burning sulfur down from the sky on Sodom and Gomorrah. 25 So the Lord destroyed those cities. He also destroyed the whole Jordan Valley, everyone living in the cities and even all the plants.

19:22 Zoar This name sounds like the Hebrew word for "little."

26 At that point Lot's wife looked back.

When she did, she became a pillar of salt.

27 Early the next morning, Abraham got up and went to the place where he had stood before the Lord. 28 Abraham looked down toward Sodom and Gomorrah and all the Jordan Valley. He saw smoke rising from the land. It was like smoke from a furnace.

29 God destroyed the cities in the valley. But he remembered what Abraham had asked. So God saved Lot's life. But he destroyed the city where Lot had lived.

Lot and His Daughters

30 Lot was afraid to continue living in Zoar. So he and his two daughters went to live in the mountains.

They lived in a cave there.

31 One day the older daughter said to the younger,

"Our father is old. Everywhere on the earth women and men marry. But there are no men around here for us to marry. 32 Let's get our father drunk. Then we can have sexual relations with him. We can use our father to have children. That way we can continue our family."

33 That night the two girls got their father drunk. Then the older daughter went and had sexual relations with him. But Lot did not know when she lay down or when she got up.

34 The next day the older daughter said to the younger,

"Last night I had sexual relations with my father. Let's get him drunk again tonight. Then you can go and have sexual relations with him, too. In this way we can use our father to have children to continue our family."

35 So that night they got their father drunk again. Then the younger daughter went and had sexual relations with him. Again, Lot did not know when she lay down or when she got up.

36 So both of Lot's daughters became pregnant by their father. 37 The older daughter gave birth to a son. She named him Moab. Moab is the ancestor of all the Moabite people who are still living today.

38 The younger daughter also gave birth to a son. She named him Ben-Ammi. He is the father of all the Ammonite people who are still living today.

Chapter

20

Abraham and Abimelech

1 Abraham left Hebron and traveled to southern Canaan. He stayed awhile between Kadesh and Shur. Then he moved to Gerar.

2 Abraham told people that his wife Sarah was his sister. Abimelech king of Gerar heard this.

So he sent some servants to take her.

3 But one night God spoke to Abimelech in a dream. God said,

"You will die. That woman you took is married."

4 But Abimelech had not slept with Sarah. So he said,

"Lord, would you destroy an innocent nation? 5 Abraham himself told me, 'This woman is my sister.' And she also said, 'He is my brother.' I am innocent. I did not know I was doing anything wrong."

6 Then God said to Abimelech in the dream,

"Yes, I know that you did not realize what you were doing. So I did not allow you to sin against me. I did not allow you to sleep with her. 7 Give Abraham his wife back. He is a prophet.[d] He will pray for you, and you will not die. But if you do not give Sarah back, you will die. And all your family will surely die."

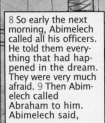

8 So early the next morning, Abimelech called all his officers. He told them everything that had happened in the dream. They were very much afraid. 9 Then Abimelech called Abraham to him. Abimelech said,

"What have you done to us? What wrong did I do against you? Why did you bring this trouble to my kingdom? You should not have done these things to me.

10 What were you thinking that caused you to do this?"

11 Then Abraham answered,

"I thought no one in this place respected God. I thought someone would kill me to get Sarah. 12 And it is true that she is my sister. She is the daughter of my father. But she is not the daughter of my mother. 13 God told me to leave my father's house and wander in many different places. When that happened, I told Sarah, 'You must do a special favor for me. Everywhere we go tell people I am your brother.' "

14 Then Abimelech gave Abraham some sheep, cattle and male and female slaves. Abimelech also gave Sarah, his wife, back to him. 15 And Abimelech said,

"Look around you at my land. You may live anywhere you want."

16 Abimelech said to Sarah,

"I gave your brother Abraham 25 pounds of silver. I did this to make up for any wrong that people may think about you. I want everyone to know that you are innocent."

17 Then Abraham prayed to God. And God healed Abimelech, his wife and his servant girls. Now they could have children. 18 The Lord had kept all the women in Abimelech's house from having children. This was God's punishment on Abimelech for taking Abraham's wife Sarah.

Chapter

21

A Baby for Sarah

1 The Lord cared for Sarah as he had said. He did for her what he had promised. 2 Sarah became pregnant. And she gave birth to a son for Abraham in his old age. Everything happened at the time God had said it would.

3 Abraham named his son Isaac. Sarah gave birth to this son of Abraham.

4 Abraham circumcised[d] Isaac when he was eight days old as God had commanded. 5 Abraham was 100 years old when his son Isaac was born.

6 And Sarah said,

"God has made me laugh.[n] Everyone who hears about this will laugh with me.

7 No one thought that I would be able to have Abraham's child. But I have given Abraham a son while he is old."

21:6 laugh The Hebrew words for "he laughed" and "Isaac" sound the same.

Hagar and Ishmael

8 Isaac grew and became old enough to eat food. At that time Abraham gave a great feast.

9 But Sarah saw Ishmael making fun of Isaac. (Ishmael was the son of Abraham by Hagar, Sarah's Egyptian slave.) 10 So Sarah said to Abraham,

"Throw out this slave woman and her son. When we die, our son Isaac will inherit everything we have. I don't want her son to inherit any of our things."

11 This troubled Abraham very much because Ishmael was also his son.

12 But God said to Abraham,

"Don't be troubled about the boy and the slave woman. Do whatever Sarah tells you. The descendants[d] I promised you will be from Isaac. 13 I will also make the descendants of Ishmael into a great nation. I will do this because he is your son, too."

14 Early the next morning Abraham took some food and a leather bag full of water. He gave them to Hagar and sent her away. Hagar carried these things and her son.

She went and wandered in the desert of Beersheba.

Genesis 21:15-24

15 Later, all the water was gone from the bag. So Hagar put her son under a bush.

16 Then she went away a short distance and sat down. Hagar thought,

"My son will die. I cannot watch this happen."

She sat there and began to cry. 17 God heard the boy crying. And God's angel called to Hagar from heaven. He said,

"What is wrong, Hagar? Don't be afraid! God has heard the boy crying there. 18 Help the boy up. Take him by the hand. I will make his descendants into a great nation."

19 Then God showed Hagar a well of water. So she went to the well and filled her bag with water. Then she gave the boy a drink.

20 God was with the boy as he grew up. Ishmael lived in the desert. He learned to shoot with a bow very well. 21 He lived in the Desert of Paran. His mother found a wife for him in Egypt.

Abraham's Bargain with Abimelech

22 Then Abimelech came with Phicol, the commander of Abimelech's army. They said to Abraham,

"God is with you in everything you do. 23 So make a promise to me here before God. Promise that you will be fair with me and my children and my descendants.[d] Be kind to me and to this land where you have lived as a stranger. Be as kind to me as I have been to you."

24 And Abraham said,

"I promise."

25 Then Abraham complained to Abimelech about Abimelech's servants. They had captured a well of water. 26 But Abimelech said,

"I don't know who did this. You never told me about this before today."

27 Then Abraham gave Abimelech some sheep and cattle. And they made an agreement.

28 Abraham also put seven female lambs in front of Abimelech. 29 Abimelech asked Abraham,

"Why did you put these seven female lambs by themselves?"

30 Abraham answered,

"Accept these lambs from me. That will prove that you believe I dug this well."

31 So that place was called Beersheba" because they made a promise to each other there.

32 So Abraham and Abimelech made an agreement at Beersheba. Then Abimelech and Phicol, the commander of his army, went back to the land of the Philistines.

33 Abraham planted a tamarisk tree at Beersheba. There Abraham prayed to the Lord, the God who lives forever.

34 And Abraham lived as a stranger in the land of the Philistines for a long time.

Chapter

22

God Tests Abraham

1 After these things God tested Abraham's faith. God said to him,

"Abraham!"

And he answered,

"Here I am."

2 Then God said,

"Take your only son, Isaac, the son you love. Go to the land of Moriah.

21:31 **Beersheba** This name means "well of the promise" or "well of seven."

49

Genesis 22:3-8

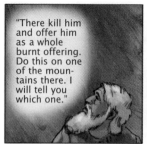

"There kill him and offer him as a whole burnt offering. Do this on one of the mountains there. I will tell you which one."

3 Early in the morning Abraham got up and saddled his donkey. He took Isaac and two servants with him.

He cut the wood for the sacrifice.

Then they went to the place God had told them to go.

4 On the third day Abraham looked up and saw the place in the distance.

5 He said to his servants,

"Stay here with the donkey. My son and I will go over there and worship. Then we will come back to you."

6 Abraham took the wood for the sacrifice and gave it to his son to carry. Abraham took the knife and the fire. So Abraham and his son went on together.

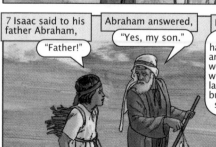

7 Isaac said to his father Abraham,

"Father!"

Abraham answered, "Yes, my son."

Isaac said,

"We have the fire and the wood. But where is the lamb we will burn as a sacrifice?"

8 Abraham answered,

"God will give us the lamb for the sacrifice, my son."

So Abraham and his son went on together. 9 They came to the place God had told him about. There, Abraham built an altar. He laid the wood on it.

Then he tied up his son Isaac.

And he laid Isaac on the wood on the altar.

10 Then Abraham took his knife and was about to kill his son.

11 But the angel of the Lord called to him from heaven. The angel said,

"Abraham! Abraham!"

Abraham answered,

"Yes."

12 The angel said,

"Don't kill your son or hurt him in any way. Now I can see that you respect God. I see that you have not kept your son, your only son, from me."

13 Then Abraham looked up and saw a male sheep. Its horns were caught in a bush.

So Abraham went and took the sheep and killed it. He offered it as a whole burnt offering to God. Abraham's son was saved.

14 So Abraham named that place The Lord Gives. Even today people say, "On the mountain of the Lord it will be given."

15 The angel of the Lord called to Abraham from heaven a second time. 16 The angel said,

"The Lord says, 'You did not keep back your son, your only son, from me. Because you did this, I make you this promise by my own name: 17 I will surely bless you and give you many descendants.[d] They will be as many as the stars in the sky and the sand on the seashore. And they will capture the cities of their enemies. 18 Through your descendants all the nations on the earth will be blessed. This is because you obeyed me.' "

51

Genesis 22:19–23:6

19 Then Abraham returned to his servants.

They all traveled back to Beersheba, and Abraham stayed there.

20 After these things happened, someone told Abraham:

"Your brother Nahor and his wife Milcah have children now. 21 The first son is Uz. The second son is Buz. The third son is Kemuel (the father of Aram). 22 Then there are Kesed, Hazo, Pildash, Jidlaph and Bethuel."

23 Bethuel became the father of Rebekah. Milcah was the mother of these eight sons, and Nahor was the father. Nahor was Abraham's brother. 24 Also Nahor had four other sons by his slave woman[d] Reumah. Their names were Tebah, Gaham, Tahash and Maacah.

Chapter 23

Sarah Dies

1 Sarah lived to be 127 years old. 2 She died in Kiriath Arba (that is, Hebron) in the land of Canaan. Abraham was very sad and cried because of her.

3 After a while Abraham got up from the side of his wife's body. And he went to talk to the Hittites. He said,

4 "I am only a stranger and a foreigner here. Sell me some of your land so that I can bury my dead wife."

5 The Hittites answered Abraham,

6 "Sir, you are a great leader among us. You may have the best place we have to bury your dead. You may have any of our burying places that you want. None of us will stop you from burying your dead wife."

x

52

7 Abraham rose and bowed to the people of the land, the Hittites. 8 Abraham said to them,

"If you truly want to help me bury my dead wife here, speak to Ephron for me. He is the son of Zohar. 9 Ask him to sell me the cave of Machpelah. It is at the edge of his field. I will pay him the full price. You can be the witnesses that I am buying it as a burial place."

10 Ephron was sitting among the Hittites at the city gate. Ephron answered Abraham,

11 "No, sir. I will give you the land and the cave that is in it. I will give it to you with these people as witnesses. Bury your dead wife."

12 Then Abraham bowed down before the Hittites.

13 He said to Ephron before all the people,

"Please let me pay you the full price for the field. Accept my money, and I will bury my dead there."

14 Ephron answered Abraham,

15 "Sir, the land is worth ten pounds of silver. But I won't argue with you over the price. Take the land, and bury your dead wife."

16 Abraham agreed and paid Ephron in front of the Hittite witnesses. Abraham weighed out the full price: ten pounds of silver. They counted the weight as the traders normally did.

17-18 So Ephron's field in Machpelah, east of Mamre, was sold.

Abraham became the owner of the field, the cave in it and all the trees that were in the field. The sale was made at the city gate, with the Hittites as witnesses.

19 After this, Abraham buried his wife Sarah in the cave. It was in that field of Machpelah, near Mamre. (Mamre was later called Hebron in the land of Canaan.) 20 Abraham bought the field and the cave on it from the Hittites. He used it as a burying place.

Chapter

24

A Wife for Isaac

1 Abraham was now very old. The Lord had blessed him in every way. 2 Abraham's oldest servant was in charge of everything Abraham owned. Abraham called that servant to him and said,

"Put your hand under my leg.ⁿ 3 Make a promise to me before the Lord, the God of heaven and earth. Don't get a wife for my son from the Canaanite girls who live around here. 4 Instead, go back to my country, to the land of my relatives. Get a wife for my son Isaac from there."

5 The servant said to him,

"What if this woman does not want to return with me to this land? Then, should I take your son with me back to your homeland?"

24:2 Put . . . leg. This showed that a person would keep the promise.

54

6 Abraham said to him,

"No! Don't take my son back there. 7 The Lord is the God of heaven. He brought me from the home of my father and the land of my relatives. But the Lord promised me, 'I will give this land to your descendants.'ᵈ The Lord will send his angel before you. The angel will help you get a wife for my son there. 8 But if the girl won't come back with you, you will be free from this promise. But you must not take my son back there."

9 So the servant put his hand under his master's leg. He made a promise to Abraham about this.

10 The servant took ten of Abraham's camels and left. He carried with him many different kinds of beautiful gifts. He went to Northwest Mesopotamia to Nahor's city.

11 He made the camels kneel down at the well outside the city. It was in the evening when the women come out to get water. 12 The servant said,

"Lord, you are the God of my master Abraham. Allow me to find a wife for his son today. Please show this kindness to my master Abraham. 13 Here I am, standing by the spring of water. The girls from the city are coming out to get water.

14 I will say to one of the girls, 'Please put your jar down so I can drink.' Then let her say, 'Drink, and I will also give water to your camels.' If that happens, I will know she is the right one for your servant Isaac. And I will know that you have shown kindness to my master."

15 Before the servant had finished praying, Rebekah came out of the city. She was the daughter of Bethuel. (Bethuel was the son of Milcah and Nahor, Abraham's brother.) Rebekah was carrying her water jar on her shoulder.

Genesis 24:16-23

16 She was very pretty. She was a virgin;[d] she had never had sexual relations with a man.

She went down to the spring and filled her jar. Then she came back up.

17 The servant ran to her and said,

"Please give me a little water from your jar."

18 Rebekah said, "Drink, sir."

She quickly lowered the jar from her shoulder and gave him a drink.

19 After he finished drinking, Rebekah said,

"I will also pour some water for your camels."

20 So she quickly poured all the water from her jar into the drinking trough for the camels. Then she kept running to the well until she had given all the camels enough to drink.

21 The servant quietly watched her. He wanted to be sure the Lord had made his trip successful.

22 After the camels had finished drinking, he gave Rebekah a gold ring weighing one-fifth of an ounce. He also gave her two gold arm bracelets weighing about four ounces each. 23 The servant asked,

"Who is your father? Is there a place in his house for me and my men to spend the night?"

24 Rebekah answered,

"My father is Bethuel. He is the son of Milcah and Nahor."

25 Then she said,

"And, yes, we have straw for your camels. We have a place for you to spend the night."

26 The servant bowed and worshiped the Lord.

27 He said,

"Blessed is the Lord, the God of my master Abraham. The Lord has been kind and truthful to him. He has led me to my master's relatives."

28 Then Rebekah ran and told her mother's family about all these things.

29 She had a brother named Laban. He ran out to Abraham's servant, who was still at the spring. 30 Laban had heard what she had said. And he had seen the ring and the bracelets on his sister's arms. So he ran out to the well. And there was the man standing by the camels at the spring.

31 Laban said,

"Sir, you are welcome to come in. You don't have to stand outside. I have prepared the house for you and also a place for your camels."

32 So Abraham's servant went into the house. Laban unloaded the camels and gave them straw and food. Then Laban gave water to Abraham's servant so he and the men with him could wash their feet.

Genesis 24:33-39

33 Then Laban gave the servant food. But the servant said,

"I will not eat until I have told you why I came."

So Laban said,

"Then tell us."

34 He said,

"I am Abraham's servant. 35 The Lord has greatly blessed my master in everything. My master has become a rich man. The Lord has given him many flocks of sheep and herds of cattle. He has given Abraham silver and gold, male and female servants, camels and horses. 36 Sarah, my master's wife, gave birth to a son when she was old. My master has given everything he owns to that son. 37 My master had me make a promise to him. He said, 'Don't get a wife for my son from the Canaanite girls who live around here. 38 Instead you must go to my father's people and to my family. There you must get a wife for my son.' 39 I said to my master, 'What if the woman will not come back with me?'

40 "But he said, 'I serve the Lord. He will send his angel with you and will help you. You will get a wife for my son from my family and my father's people. 41 Then you will be free from the promise. Or if they will not give you a wife for my son, you will be free from this promise.'

42 "Today I came to this spring. I said, 'Lord, God of my master Abraham, please make my trip successful. 43 Look, I am standing by this spring of water. I will wait for a young woman to come out to get water. Then I will say, "Please give me water from your jar to drink." 44 Then let her say, "Drink this water. I will also get water for your camels." By this I will know the Lord has chosen her for my master's son.'

45 "Before I finished my silent prayer, Rebekah came out of the city. She had her water jar on her shoulder. She went down to the spring and got water. I said to her, 'Please give me a drink.' 46 She quickly lowered the jar from her shoulder. She said, 'Drink this. I will also get water for your camels.' So I drank, and she gave water to my camels also.

47 Then I asked her, 'Who is your father?' She answered, 'My father is Bethuel son of Milcah and Nahor.' Then I put the ring in her nose and the bracelets on her arms. 48 At that time I bowed my head and thanked the Lord. I praised the Lord, the God of my master Abraham. I thanked him because he led me on the right road to get the granddaughter of my master's brother for his son. 49 Now, tell me, will you be kind and truthful to my master? And if not, tell me so. Then I will know what I should do."

Genesis 24:50-57

50 Laban and Bethuel answered,

"This is clearly from the Lord. We cannot change what must happen. 51 Rebekah is yours. Take her and go. Let her marry your master's son as the Lord has commanded."

52 When Abraham's servant heard these words, he bowed face-down on the ground before the Lord.

53 Then the servant gave Rebekah gold and silver jewelry and clothes. He also gave expensive gifts to her brother and mother.

54 The servant and the men with him ate and drank. And they spent the night there.

When they got up the next morning, the servant said,

"Now let me go back to my master."

55 Rebekah's mother and her brother said,

"Let Rebekah stay with us at least ten days. After that she may go."

56 But the servant said to them,

"Do not make me wait. The Lord has made my trip successful. Now let me go back to my master."

57 Rebekah's brother and mother said,

"We will call Rebekah and ask her what she wants to do."

58 They called her and asked her,

"Do you want to go with this man now?"

She said,

"Yes, I do."

59 So they allowed Rebekah and her nurse to go with Abraham's servant and his men. 60 They blessed Rebekah and said,

"Our sister, may you be the mother of thousands of people. And may your descendants[d] capture the cities of their enemies."

61 Then Rebekah and her servant girls got on the camels and followed the servant and his men. So the servant took Rebekah and left.

62 At this time Isaac had left Beer Lahai Roi. He was living in southern Canaan. 63 One evening he went out to the field to think. As he looked up, he saw camels coming.

64 Rebekah looked and saw Isaac. Then she jumped down from the camel. 65 She asked the servant,

"Who is that man walking in the field to meet us?"

The servant answered,

"That is my master."

So Rebekah covered her face with her veil.

66 The servant told Isaac everything that had happened.

67 Then Isaac brought Rebekah into the tent of Sarah, his mother. And she became his wife. Isaac loved her very much.

So he was comforted after his mother's death.

Chapter

25

Abraham's Family

1 Abraham married again. His new wife was Keturah. 2 She gave birth to Zimran, Jokshan, Medan, Midian, Ishbak and Shuah. 3 Jokshan was the father of Sheba and Dedan. Dedan's descendants[d] were the people of Assyria, Letush and Leum. 4 The sons of Midian were Ephah, Epher, Hanoch, Abida and Eldaah. All these were descendants of Keturah. 5 Abraham left everything he owned to Isaac. 6 But before Abraham died, he did give gifts to the sons of his other wives. Abraham sent them to the East to be away from Isaac.

7 Abraham lived to be 175 years old. 8 He breathed his last breath and died at an old age. He had lived a long and satisfying life. 9 His sons Isaac and Ishmael buried him in the cave of Machpelah. This cave is in the field of Ephron east of Mamre. Ephron was the son of Zohar the Hittite. 10 This is the same field that Abraham had bought from the Hittites. Abraham was buried there with his wife Sarah. 11 After Abraham died, God blessed his son Isaac. Isaac was now living at Beer Lahai Roi.

12 This is the family history of Ishmael, Abraham's son. (Hagar, Sarah's Egyptian servant, was Ishmael's mother.) 13 These are the names of Ishmael's sons in the order they were born. The first son was Nebaioth. Then came Kedar, Adbeel, Mibsam, 14 Mishma, Dumah, Massa, 15 Hadad, Tema, Jetur, Naphish and Kedemah. 16 These were Ishmael's sons. And these are the names of the tribal leaders. They are listed according to their settlements and camps. 17 Ishmael lived 137 years. Then he breathed his last breath and died. 18 Ishmael's descendants lived from Havilah to Shur. This is east of Egypt stretching toward Assyria. Ishmael's descendants often attacked the descendants of his brothers.

Isaac's Family

19 This is the family history of Isaac. Abraham had a son named Isaac. 20 When Isaac was 40 years old, he married Rebekah. Rebekah was from Northwest Mesopotamia. She was Bethuel's daughter and the sister of Laban the Aramean.

21 Isaac's wife could not have children. So Isaac prayed to the Lord for her. The Lord heard Isaac's prayer, and Rebekah became pregnant.

22 While she was pregnant, the babies struggled inside her. She asked,

"Why is this happening to me?"

Then she went to get an answer from the Lord. 23 The Lord said to her,

"Two nations are in your body. Two groups of people will be taken from you. One group will be stronger than the other. The older will serve the younger."

Genesis 25:24-34

24 And when the time came, Rebekah gave birth to twins. 25 The first baby was born red. His skin was like a hairy robe. So he was named Esau.[n] 26 When the second baby was born, he was holding on to Esau's heel. So that baby was named Jacob.[n] Isaac was 60 years old when they were born.

27 When the boys grew up, Esau became a skilled hunter. He loved to be out in the fields.

But Jacob was a quiet man. He stayed among the tents.

28 Isaac loved Esau. Esau hunted the wild animals that Isaac enjoyed eating. But Rebekah loved Jacob.

29 One day Jacob was boiling a pot of vegetable soup. Esau came in from hunting in the fields. He was weak from hunger. 30 So Esau said to Jacob,

"Let me eat some of that red soup. I am weak with hunger."

(That is why people call him Edom.[n]) 31 But Jacob said,

"You must sell me your rights as the first-born son."[n]

32 Esau said,

"I am almost dead from hunger. If I die, all of my father's wealth will not help me."

33 But Jacob said,

"First, promise me that you will give it to me."

So Esau made a promise to Jacob. In this way he sold his part of their father's wealth to Jacob. 34 Then Jacob gave Esau bread and vegetable soup. Esau ate and drank and then left. So Esau showed how little he cared about his rights as the firstborn son.

25:25 Esau This name may mean "hairy." **25:26 Jacob** This name sounds like the Hebrew word for "heel." "Grabbing someone's heel" is a Hebrew saying for tricking someone. **25:30 Edom** This name sounds like the Hebrew word for "red." **25:31 rights . . . son** Usually the firstborn son had a high rank in the family. The firstborn son usually became the new head of the family.

Chapter 26

1 Once there was a time of hunger in the land. This was besides the time of hunger that happened during Abraham's life. So Isaac went to the town of Gerar. He went to see Abimelech king of the Philistines.

2 The Lord appeared to Isaac and said,

"Don't go down to Egypt. Live in the land where I tell you to live. 3 Stay in this land, and I will be with you. I will bless you. I will give you and your descendants[d] all these lands. I will keep the agreement I made to Abraham your father. 4 I will give you many descendants. They will be as hard to count as the stars in the sky. And I will give them all these lands. Through your descendants all the nations on the earth will be blessed. 5 I will do this because your father Abraham obeyed me. He did what I said. He obeyed my commands, my teachings and my rules."

6 So Isaac stayed in Gerar. 7 Isaac's wife Rebekah was very beautiful. The men of that place asked Isaac about her. Isaac said,

"She is my sister."

He was afraid to tell them she was his wife. He thought they might kill him so they could have her. 8 Isaac lived there a long time. One day as Abimelech king of the Philistines looked out his window, he saw Isaac. Isaac was holding his wife Rebekah tenderly.

9 Abimelech called for Isaac and said,

"This woman is your wife. Why did you say she was your sister?"

Isaac said to him,

"I was afraid you would kill me so you could have her."

10 Abimelech said,

"What have you done to us? One of our men might have had sexual relations with your wife. Then we would have been guilty of a great sin."

11 So Abimelech warned everyone. He said,

"Anyone who touches this man or his wife will be put to death."

Isaac Becomes Rich

12 Isaac planted seed in that land. And that year he gathered a great harvest. The Lord blessed him very much. 13 Isaac became rich. He gathered more wealth until he became a very rich man. 14 He had many slaves and many flocks and herds. The Philistines envied him.

15 So they stopped up all the wells the servants of Isaac's father Abraham had dug.

(They had dug them when Abraham was alive.) The Philistines filled those wells with dirt.

16 And Abimelech said to Isaac,

"Leave our country. You have become much more powerful than we are."

17 So Isaac left that place. He camped in the Valley of Gerar and lived there.

18 Long before this time Abraham had dug many wells. After Abraham died, the Philistines filled them with dirt. So Isaac dug those wells again. He gave them the same names his father had given them.

19 Isaac's servants dug a well in the valley. From it a spring of water flowed. 20 But the men who herded sheep in Gerar argued with Isaac's servants. They said,

"This water is ours."

So Isaac named that well Argue because they argued with him.

21 Then Isaac's servants dug another well. The people also argued about it. So Isaac named that well Fight. 22 Isaac moved from there and dug another well. No one argued about this one. So he named that well Room Enough. Isaac said,

"Now the Lord has made room for us. We will be successful in this land."

23 From there Isaac went to Beersheba. 24 The Lord appeared to Isaac that night. The Lord said,

"I am the God of your father Abraham. Don't be afraid because I am with you. I will bless you and give you many descendants.[d] I will do this because of my servant Abraham."

25 So Isaac built an altar and worshiped the Lord there. He made a camp there, and his servants dug a well.

Genesis 26:26–27:1

26 Abimelech came from Gerar to see Isaac. Abimelech brought with him Ahuzzath, who advised him, and Phicol, the commander of his army. 27 Isaac asked them,

"Why have you come to see me? You were my enemy. You forced me to leave your country."

28 They answered,

"Now we know that the Lord is with you. We will make a promise to you. And we would like you to make one to us. We would like to make an agreement with you. 29 We did not hurt you. So promise you will not hurt us. And we were good to you, and we sent you away in peace. Now the Lord has blessed you."

30 So Isaac prepared food for them, and they all ate and drank.

31 Early the next morning the men made a promise to each other. Then Isaac sent them away, and they left in peace.

32 That day Isaac's servants came and told him about the well they had dug. They said,

"We found water in that well."

33 So Isaac named it Shibah[n] and that city is still called Beersheba even now.

34 When Esau was 40 years old, he married two Hittite women. One was Judith daughter of Beeri. The other was Basemath daughter of Elon. 35 These women brought much sorrow to Isaac and Rebekah.

Chapter 27

Jacob Tricks Isaac

1 When Isaac was old, his eyes were not good. He could not see clearly. One day he called his older son Esau to him. Isaac said,

"Son."

Esau answered,

"Here I am."

26:33 Shibah This name sounds like the Hebrew words for "seven" and "promise."

68

2 Isaac said,

"I am old. I don't know when I might die. 3 So take your bow and arrows, and go hunting in the field. Kill an animal for me to eat. 4 Prepare the tasty food that I love. Bring it to me, and I will eat. Then I will bless you before I die."

5 So Esau went out in the field to hunt. Rebekah was listening as Isaac said this to his son Esau.

6 Rebekah said to her son Jacob,

"Listen, I heard your father talking to your brother Esau. 7 Your father said, 'Kill an animal. Prepare some tasty food for me to eat. Then I will bless you before the Lord before I die.'

8 So obey me, my son. Do what I tell you.

9 Go out to our goats and bring me two young ones. I will prepare them just the way your father likes them. 10 Then you will take the food to your father. And he will bless you before he dies."

11 But Jacob said to his mother Rebekah,

"My brother Esau is a hairy man. I am smooth! 12 If my father touches me, he will know I am not Esau. Then he will not bless me. He will place a curse on me because I tried to trick him."

13 So Rebekah said to him,

"If your father puts a curse on you, I will accept the blame. Just do what I said. Go and get the goats for me."

Genesis 27:14-23

14 So Jacob went out and got two goats and brought them to his mother. Then she cooked them in the special way Isaac enjoyed.

15 She took the best clothes of her older son Esau that were in the house. She put them on the younger son Jacob.

16 She took the skins of the goats. And she put them on Jacob's hands and neck.

17 Then she gave Jacob the tasty food and the bread she had made. 18 Jacob went in to his father and said,

"Father."

And his father said,

"Yes, my son. Who are you?"

19 Jacob said to him,

"I am Esau, your first son. I have done what you told me. Now sit up and eat some meat of the animal I hunted for you. Then bless me."

20 But Isaac asked his son,

"How did you find and kill the animal so quickly?"

Jacob answered,

"Because the Lord your God led me to find it."

21 Then Isaac said to Jacob,

"Come near so I can touch you, my son. If I can touch you, I will know if you are really my son Esau."

22 So Jacob came near to Isaac his father. Isaac touched him and said,

"Your voice sounds like Jacob's voice. But your hands are hairy like the hands of Esau."

23 Isaac did not know it was Jacob, because his hands were hairy like Esau's hands. So Isaac blessed Jacob.

70

24 Isaac asked,

"Are you really my son Esau?"

Jacob answered,

"Yes, I am."

25 Then Isaac said,

"Bring me the food. I will eat it and bless you."

So Jacob gave him the food, and Isaac ate. Jacob gave him wine, and he drank.

26 Then Isaac said to him,

"My son, come near and kiss me."

27 So Jacob went to his father and kissed him. Isaac smelled Esau's clothes and blessed him. Isaac said,

"The smell of my son is like the smell of the field that the Lord has blessed.

28 May God give you plenty of rain and good soil. Then you will have plenty of grain and wine. 29 May nations serve you. May peoples bow down to you. May you be master over your brothers. May your mother's sons bow down to you. May everyone who curses you be cursed. And may everyone who blesses you be blessed."

30 Isaac finished blessing Jacob. Then, just as Jacob left his father Isaac, Esau came in from hunting.

31 Esau also prepared some tasty food and brought it to his father. He said,

"Father, rise and eat the food that your son killed for you. Then bless me."

Genesis 27:32-38

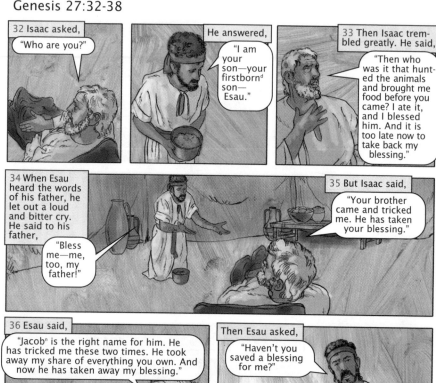

32 Isaac asked,

"Who are you?"

He answered,

"I am your son—your firstborn[d] son—Esau."

33 Then Isaac trembled greatly. He said,

"Then who was it that hunted the animals and brought me food before you came? I ate it, and I blessed him. And it is too late now to take back my blessing."

34 When Esau heard the words of his father, he let out a loud and bitter cry. He said to his father,

"Bless me—me, too, my father!"

35 But Isaac said,

"Your brother came and tricked me. He has taken your blessing."

36 Esau said,

"Jacob[n] is the right name for him. He has tricked me these two times. He took away my share of everything you own. And now he has taken away my blessing."

Then Esau asked,

"Haven't you saved a blessing for me?"

37 Isaac answered,

"I gave Jacob the power to be master over you. And all his brothers will be his servants. And I kept him strong with grain and wine. There is nothing left to give you, my son."

38 But Esau continued,

"Do you have only one blessing, Father? Bless me, too, Father!"

27:36 Jacob This name sounds like the Hebrew word for "heel." "Grabbing someone's heel" is a Hebrew saying for tricking someone.

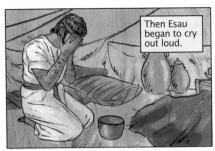

Then Esau began to cry out loud.

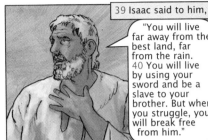

39 Isaac said to him,

"You will live far away from the best land, far from the rain. 40 You will live by using your sword and be a slave to your brother. But when you struggle, you will break free from him."

41 After that Esau hated Jacob because of the blessing from Isaac. Esau thought to himself,

"My father will soon die, and I will be sad for him. After that I will kill Jacob."

42 Rebekah heard about Esau's plan to kill Jacob.

So she sent for Jacob. She said to him,

"Listen, your brother Esau is comforting himself by planning to kill you. 43 So, son, do what I say. My brother Laban is living in Haran. Go to him at once! 44 Stay with him for a while, until your brother is not so angry.

45 In time, your brother will not be angry. He will forget what you did to him. Then I will send a servant to bring you back. I don't want to lose both of my sons on the same day."

46 Then Rebekah said to Isaac,

"I am tired of Hittite women. If Jacob marries one of these Hittite women here in this land, I want to die."

Genesis 28:1-9

Chapter 28

Jacob Searches for a Wife

1 Isaac called Jacob and blessed him. Then Isaac commanded him,

"You must not marry a Canaanite woman. 2 Go to the house of Bethuel, your mother's father, in Northwest Mesopotamia. Laban, your mother's brother, lives there. Marry one of his daughters. 3 May God All-Powerful bless you and give you many children. May you become the father of many peoples. 4 May the Lord give you and your descendants[d] the blessing of Abraham. Then you may own the land where you are now living as a stranger. This is the land God gave to Abraham."

5 So Isaac sent Jacob to Northwest Mesopotamia. Jacob went to Laban, the brother of Rebekah. Bethuel, the Aramean, was the father of Laban and Rebekah. And Rebekah was the mother of Jacob and Esau.

6 Esau learned that Isaac had blessed Jacob and sent him to Northwest Mesopotamia. Jacob went to find a wife there. Esau also learned that Isaac had commanded Jacob not to marry a Canaanite woman. 7 And Esau learned that Jacob had obeyed his father and mother. He had gone to Northwest Mesopotamia. 8 So Esau saw that his father Isaac did not want his sons to marry Canaanite women. 9 Now Esau already had wives. But he went to Ishmael son of Abraham. And he married Mahalath, Ishmael's daughter. Mahalath was the sister of Nebaioth.

Jacob's Dream at Bethel

10 Jacob left Beersheba and set out for Haran. 11 He came to a place and spent the night there because the sun had set.

He found a stone there and laid his head on it to go to sleep.

12 Jacob dreamed that there was a ladder resting on the earth and reaching up into heaven. And he saw angels of God going up and coming down the ladder. 13 And then Jacob saw the Lord standing above the ladder. The Lord said,

"I am the Lord, the God of Abraham, your grandfather. And I am the God of Isaac. I will give you and your descendants^d the land on which you are now sleeping. 14 Your descendants will be as many as the dust of the earth. They will spread west and east, north and south. All the families of the earth will be blessed through you and your descendants. 15 I am with you, and I will protect you everywhere you go. And I will bring you back to this land. I will not leave you until I have done what I have promised you."

16 Then Jacob woke from his sleep. He said,

"Surely the Lord is in this place. But I did not know it."

17 Jacob was afraid. He said,

"This place frightens me! It is surely the house of God and the gate of heaven."

18 Jacob rose early in the morning. He took the stone he had slept on and set it up on its end. Then he poured olive oil on the top of it. 19 At first, the name of that city was Luz. But Jacob named it Bethel."

20 Then Jacob made a promise. He said,

"I want God to be with me and protect me on this journey. I want God to give me food to eat and clothes to wear. 21 Then I will be able to return in peace to my father's house. If the Lord does these things, he will be my God. 22 This stone which I have set up on its end will be the house of God. And I will give God one-tenth of all he gives me."

Chapter 29

Jacob Arrives in Northwest Mesopotamia

1 Then Jacob continued his journey. He came to the land of the people of the East. 2 He looked and saw a well in the field. Three flocks of sheep were lying nearby, because they drank water from this well.

A large stone covered the mouth of the well.

3 All the flocks would gather there. The shepherds would roll the stone away from the well and water the sheep. Then they would put the stone back in its place.

28:19 Bethel This name means "house of God."

4 Jacob said to the shepherds there,

"My brothers, where are you from?"

They answered,

"We are from Haran."

5 Then Jacob asked,

"Do you know Laban grandson of Nahor?"

They answered,

"We know him."

6 Then Jacob asked,

"How is he?"

They answered,

"He is well. Look, his daughter Rachel is coming now with his sheep."

7 Jacob said,

"But look, it is still the middle part of the day. It is not time for the sheep to be gathered for the night. So give them water and let them go back into the pasture."

8 But they said,

"We cannot do that until all the flocks are gathered. Then we will roll away the stone from the mouth of the well and water the sheep."

9 While Jacob was talking with the shepherds, Rachel came with her father's sheep. It was her job to take care of the sheep.

10 Then Jacob saw Laban's daughter Rachel and Laban's sheep.

So he went to the well and rolled the stone from its mouth. Then he watered Laban's sheep. Now Laban was the brother of Rebekah, Jacob's mother.

Genesis 29:11-21

11 Then Jacob kissed Rachel

and cried.

12 He told her that he was from her father's family. He said that he was the son of Rebekah.

So Rachel ran home and told her father.

13 When Laban heard the news about his sister's son Jacob, Laban ran to meet him.

Laban hugged him and kissed him and brought him to his house.

Jacob told Laban everything that had happened. 14 Then Laban said,

"You are my own flesh and blood."

Jacob Is Tricked

So Jacob stayed there a month. 15 Then Laban said to Jacob,

"You are my relative. But it is not right for you to keep on working for me without pay. What would you like me to pay you?"

16 Now Laban had two daughters. The older was Leah, and the younger was Rachel. 17 Leah had weak eyes, but Rachel was very beautiful.

18 Jacob loved Rachel. So he said to Laban,

"Let me marry your younger daughter Rachel. If you will, I will work seven years for you."

19 Laban said,

"It would be better for her to marry you than someone else. So stay here with me."

20 So Jacob worked for Laban seven years so he could marry Rachel.

But they seemed to him like just a few days. This was because he loved Rachel very much. 21 After seven years Jacob said to Laban,

"Give me Rachel so that I may marry her. The time I promised to work for you is over."

22 So Laban gave a feast for all the people there.

23 That evening Laban brought his daughter Leah to Jacob. Jacob and Leah had sexual relations together.

24 (Laban gave his slave girl Zilpah to his daughter to be her servant.) 25 In the morning Jacob saw that he had had sexual relations with Leah! He said to Laban,

"What have you done to me? I worked hard for you so that I could marry Rachel! Why did you trick me?"

26 Laban said,

"In our country we do not allow the younger daughter to marry before the older daughter. 27 But complete the full week of the marriage ceremony with Leah. I will give you Rachel to marry also. But you must serve me another seven years."

28 So Jacob did this and completed the week with Leah. Then Laban gave him his daughter Rachel as a wife.

29 (Laban gave his slave girl Bilhah to his daughter Rachel to be her servant.) 30 So Jacob had sexual relations with Rachel also. And Jacob loved Rachel more than Leah. Jacob worked for Laban for another seven years.

Jacob's Family Grows

31 The Lord saw that Jacob loved Rachel more than Leah. So the Lord made it possible for Leah to have children. But Rachel did not have any children. 32 Leah became pregnant and gave birth to a son. She named him Reuben[n] because she said,

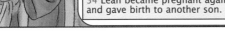

"The Lord has seen my troubles. Surely now my husband will love me."

33 Leah became pregnant again and gave birth to another son. She named him Simeon.[n] She said,

"The Lord has heard that I am not loved. So he gave me this son."

34 Leah became pregnant again and gave birth to another son.

She named him Levi.[n] Leah said,

"Now, surely my husband will be close to me. I have given him three sons."

35 Then Leah gave birth to another son. She named him Judah.[n] Leah named him this because she said,

"Now I will praise the Lord."

Then Leah stopped having children.

29:32 Reuben This name sounds like the Hebrew word for "he has seen my troubles."
29:33 Simeon This name sounds like the Hebrew word for "has heard."
29:34 Levi This name sounds like the Hebrew word for "be close to."
29:35 Judah This name sounds like the Hebrew word for "praise."

Chapter

30

1 Rachel saw that she was not giving birth to children for Jacob.

So she envied her sister Leah. Rachel said to Jacob,

"Give me children, or I'll die!"

2 Jacob became angry with her. He said,

"Can I do what only God can do? He is the one who has kept you from having children."

3 Then Rachel said, "Here is my slave girl Bilhah. Have sexual relations with her so she can give birth to a child for me. Then I can have my own family through her."

4 So Rachel gave Bilhah, her slave girl, to Jacob as a wife. And he had sexual relations with her. 5 She became pregnant and gave Jacob a son. 6 Rachel said,

"God has declared me innocent. He has listened to my prayer and has given me a son."

So Rachel named this son Dan.[n] 7 Bilhah became pregnant again and gave Jacob a second son. 8 Rachel said,

"I have struggled hard with my sister. And I have won."

So she named that son Naphtali.[n]

9 Leah saw that she had stopped having children. So she gave her slave girl Zilpah to Jacob as a wife.

10 Then Zilpah had a son. 11 Leah said,

"I am lucky."

So she named her son Gad.[n]

12 Zilpah gave birth to another son. 13 Leah said,

"I am very happy! Now women will call me happy."

So she named that son Asher.[n]

14 During the wheat harvest Reuben went into the field and found some mandrake[n] plants. He brought them to his mother Leah.

30:6 Dan This name means "he has declared innocent."
30:8 Naphtali This name sounds like the Hebrew word for "my struggle."
30:11 Gad This name may mean "lucky."
30:13 Asher This name may mean "happy."
30:14 mandrake A plant which was believed to cause a woman to become pregnant.

But Rachel said to Leah,

"Please give me some of your son's mandrakes."

15 Leah answered,

"You have already taken away my husband. Now you are trying to take away my son's mandrakes."

But Rachel answered,

"If you will give me your son's mandrakes, you may sleep with Jacob tonight."

16 When Jacob came in from the field that night, Leah went out to meet him. She said,

"You will have sexual relations with me tonight. I have paid for you with my son's mandrakes."

So Jacob slept with her that night.

17 Then God answered Leah's prayer, and she became pregnant again. She gave birth to a fifth son.

18 Leah said,

"God has given me what I paid for, because I gave my slave girl to my husband."

So Leah named her son Issachar.[n]

19 Leah became pregnant again and gave birth to a sixth son. 20 She said,

"God has given me a fine gift. Now surely Jacob will honor me, because I have given him six sons."

So Leah named the son Zebulun.[n]

21 Later Leah gave birth to a daughter. She named her Dinah. 22 Then God remembered Rachel and answered her prayer. God made it possible for her to have children. 23 She became pregnant and gave birth to a son. She said,

"God has taken away my shame."

24 She named him Joseph.[n] Rachel said,

"I wish the Lord would give me another son."

30:18 **Issachar** This name sounds like the Hebrew word for "paid for."
30:20 **Zebulun** This name sounds like the Hebrew word for "honor."
30:24 **Joseph** This name sounds like the Hebrew word for "he adds."

Jacob Tricks Laban

25 After the birth of Joseph, Jacob said to Laban,

"Now let me go to my own home and country. 26 Give me my wives and my children, and let me go. I have earned them by working for you. You know that I served you well."

27 Laban said to him,

"If I have pleased you, please stay. I know the Lord has blessed me because of you. 28 Tell me what I should pay you, and I will give it to you."

29 Jacob answered,

"You know that I have worked hard for you. Your flocks have grown while I cared for them. 30 When I came, you had little. Now you have much. Every time I did something for you, the Lord blessed you. But when will I be able to do something for my own family?"

31 Laban asked,

"Then what should I give you?"

Jacob answered,

"I don't want you to give me anything. Just do this one thing. Then I will come back and take care of your flocks. 32 Today let me go through all your flocks of white sheep and black goats. I will take every spotted or speckled lamb. I will take every black lamb and every spotted or speckled goat. That will be my pay."

33 "In the future you can easily see if I am honest. You can come to look at my flocks. If I have any goat that isn't speckled or spotted or any sheep that isn't black, you will know I stole it."

34 Laban answered,

"Agreed! We will do what you ask."

35 But that day Laban took away all the male goats that had streaks or spots. And he took all the speckled and spotted female goats (all those that had white on them). And he took all the black sheep. He told his sons to watch over them. 36 Laban took these animals to a place that was three days' journey away from Jacob. Jacob took care of all the animals that were left.
37 So Jacob cut green branches from poplar, almond and plane trees. He peeled off some of the bark so that the branches had white stripes on them. 38 He put the branches in front of the flocks at the watering places. When the animals came to drink, they also mated there. 39 So the goats mated in front of the branches. Then the young that were born were streaked, speckled or spotted. 40 Jacob separated the young animals from the others. And he made them face the streaked and dark animals in Laban's flock. Jacob kept his animals separate from Laban's.

41 When the stronger animals in the flock were mating, Jacob put the branches before their eyes. This was so the animals would mate near the branches. 42 But when the weaker animals mated, Jacob did not put the branches there. So the animals born from the weaker animals were Laban's. And the animals born from the stronger animals were Jacob's. 43 In this way Jacob became very rich. He had large flocks, many male and female servants, camels and donkeys.

Chapter

31

Jacob Runs Away

1 One day Jacob heard Laban's sons talking. They said,

"Jacob has taken everything our father owned. Jacob has become rich in this way."

2 Then Jacob noticed that Laban was not as friendly as he had been before.

3 The Lord said to Jacob,

"Go back to the land where your ancestors lived. I will be with you."

4 So Jacob told Rachel and Leah to meet him in the field where he kept his flocks. 5 He said to them,

"I have seen that your father is not as friendly with me as he used to be. But the God of my father has been with me. 6 You both know that I have worked as hard as I could for your father. 7 But he cheated me. He has changed my pay ten times. But God has not allowed your father to harm me. 8 At one time Laban said, 'You can have all the speckled goats as your pay.' After that, all the animals gave birth to speckled young ones. But then Laban said, 'You can have all the streaked goats as your pay.' After that, all the animals gave birth to streaked babies. 9 So God has taken the animals away from your father. And God has given them to me.

10 "I had a dream during the season when the animals were mating. I saw that the only male goats who were mating were streaked, speckled or spotted. 11 The angel of God spoke to me in that dream. He said, 'Jacob!' I answered, 'Yes!' 12 The angel said, 'Look! Only the streaked, speckled or spotted goats are mating. I have seen all the wrong things Laban does to you. 13 I am the God who appeared to you at Bethel. There you poured olive oil on the stone you set up on end. There you made a promise to me. Now I want you to leave here. Go back to the land where you were born.' "

14 Rachel and Leah answered Jacob,

"Our father has nothing to give us when he dies. 15 He has treated us like strangers. He sold us to you, and then he spent all of the money you paid for us. 16 God took all this wealth from our father, and now it belongs to us and our children. So you do whatever God told you to do."

17 So Jacob put his children and his wives on camels. 18 Then they began their journey back to Isaac, his father. He lived in the land of Canaan. All the flocks of animals that Jacob owned walked ahead of them. He carried everything with him that he had gotten while he lived in Northwest Mesopotamia.

19 Laban was gone to cut the wool from his sheep. While he was gone, Rachel stole the idols of false gods that belonged to him.

20 And Jacob tricked Laban the Aramean. He did not tell Laban he was leaving. 21 Jacob and his family left quickly. They crossed the Euphrates River and traveled toward the mountains of Gilead. 22 Three days later Laban learned that Jacob had run away. 23 So Laban gathered his relatives and began to chase Jacob.

After seven days Laban found him in the mountains of Gilead. 24 That night God came to Laban the Aramean in a dream.

The Lord said, "Be careful! Do not say anything to Jacob, good or bad."

The Search for the Stolen Idols

25 So Laban caught up with Jacob. Now Jacob had made his camp in the mountains. So Laban and his relatives set up their camp in the mountains of Gilead.

Genesis 31:26-35

26 Laban said to Jacob,

"What have you done? Why did you trick me? You took my daughters as if you had captured them in a war. 27 Why did you run away without telling me? Why did you trick me? Why didn't you tell me? Then I could send you away with joy and singing. There would be the music of tambourines[d] and harps. 28 You did not even let me kiss my grandchildren and my daughters good-bye. You were very foolish to do this! 29 I have the power to harm you. But last night the God of your father spoke to me. He warned me not to say anything to you, good or bad. 30 I know you want to go back to your home. But why did you steal my idols?"

31 Jacob answered Laban,

"I left without telling you, because I was afraid! I thought you would take your daughters away from me. 32 If you find anyone here who has taken your idols, he will be killed! Your relatives will be my witnesses. You may look for anything that belongs to you. Take anything that is yours."

(Now Jacob did not know that Rachel had stolen Laban's idols.)

33 So Laban looked in Jacob's tent

and in Leah's tent. He looked in the tent where the two slave women stayed.

But he did not find his idols.

When he left Leah's tent, he went into Rachel's tent.

34 Rachel had hidden the idols inside her camel's saddle. And she was sitting on them. Laban looked through the whole tent, but he did not find them. 35 Rachel said to her father,

"Father, don't be angry with me. I am not able to stand up before you. I am having my monthly period."

So Laban looked through the camp, but he did not find his idols.

36 Then Jacob became very angry. He said,

"What wrong have I done? What law have I broken to cause you to chase me? 37 You have looked through everything I own. But you have found nothing that belongs to you. If you have found anything, show it to everyone. Put it in front of your relatives and my relatives. Then let them decide which one of us is right. 38 I have worked for you now for 20 years. During all that time none of the lambs and kids died during birth. And I have not eaten any of the male sheep from your flocks. 39 Any time a sheep was killed by wild animals, I did not bring it to you. I made up for the loss myself. You made me pay for any animal that was stolen during the day or night. 40 In the daytime the sun took away my strength. At night I was cold and could not sleep. 41 I worked like a slave for you for 20 years. For the first 14 years I worked to get your two daughters. The last 6 years I worked to earn your animals. And during that time you changed my pay ten times. 42 But the God of my father was with me. He is the God of Abraham and the God of Isaac. If God had not been with me, you would have sent me away with nothing. But he saw the trouble I had and the hard work I did. And last night God corrected you."

Jacob and Laban's Agreement

43 Laban said to Jacob,

"These girls are my daughters. Their children belong to me, and these animals are mine. Everything you see here belongs to me. But I can do nothing to keep my daughters and their children. 44 Let us make an agreement. Let us set up a pile of stones to remind us of our agreement."

45 So Jacob took a large rock and set it up on its end. 46 He told his relatives to gather rocks.

So they took the rocks and piled them up. Then they ate beside the pile of rocks. 47 Laban named that place in his language A Pile to Remind Us. And Jacob gave the place the same name in Hebrew. 48 Laban said to Jacob,

"This pile of rocks will remind us of the agreement between us."

That is why the place was called A Pile to Remind Us. 49 It was also called Mizpah."

31:49 Mizpah This name sounds like the Hebrew word for "watch."

This was because Laban said,

"Let the Lord watch over us while we are separated from each other. 50 Remember that God is our witness. This is true even if no one else is around us. He will know if you harm my daughters or marry other women.

51 Here is the pile of rocks that I have put between us. And here is the rock I set up on end.

52 This pile of rocks and this rock set on end will remind us of our agreement. I will never go past this pile to hurt you. And you must never come to my side of them to hurt me.

53 The God of Abraham is the God of Nahor and the God of their ancestors. Let God punish either of us if we break this agreement."

So Jacob made a promise in the name of God. This was the God of his father Isaac.

54 Then Jacob killed an animal and offered it as a sacrifice on the mountain. And he invited his relatives to share in the meal. After they finished eating, they spent the night on the mountain.

55 Early the next morning Laban kissed his grandchildren and his daughters. He blessed them,

and then he left to return home.

Chapter

32

Jacob Meets Esau

1 When Jacob also went his way, the angels of God met him. 2 When Jacob saw them, he said,

3 Jacob's brother Esau was living in the area called Seir in the country of Edom. Jacob sent messengers to Esau.

"This is the camp of God!"

So Jacob named that place Mahanaim."

32:2 Mahanaim This name means "two camps."

4 Jacob told the messengers,

"Give this message to my master Esau: 'This is what Jacob, your servant, says: I have lived with Laban and have remained there until now. 5 I have cattle, donkeys, flocks, and male and female servants. I send this message to you and ask you to accept us.' "

6 The messengers returned to Jacob

7 Then Jacob was very afraid and worried. He divided the people who were with him into two camps. He also divided all the flocks, herds and camels into two camps. 8 Jacob thought,

and said,

"We went to your brother Esau. He is coming to meet you. And he has 400 men with him."

"Esau might come and destroy one camp. But the other camp can run away and be saved."

9 Jacob said, "God of my father Abraham! God of my father Isaac! Lord, you told me to return to my country and my family. You said that you would do good to me. 10 I am not worthy of the kindness and continual goodness you have shown me. The first time I traveled across the Jordan River, I had only my walking stick. But now I own enough to have two camps. 11 Please save me from my brother Esau. I am afraid he will come and kill all of us, even the mothers with the children. 12 You said to me, 'I will do good to you. I will make your children as many as the sand of the seashore. There will be too many to count.' "

13 Jacob stayed there for the night. He prepared a gift for Esau from what he had with him. 14 It was 200 female goats and 20 male goats, 200 female sheep and 20 male sheep. 15 There were 30 female camels and their young, 40 cows and 10 bulls, 20 female donkeys and 10 male donkeys. 16 Jacob gave each separate flock of animals to one of his servants. Then he said to them,

"Go ahead of me and keep some space between each herd."

Genesis 32:17-26

17 Jacob gave them their orders. To the servant with the first group of animals he said,

"My brother Esau will come to you. He will ask you, 'Whose servant are you? Where are you going? Whose animals are these?' 18 Then you will answer, 'These animals belong to your servant Jacob. He sent them as a gift to you my master, Esau. And Jacob also is coming behind us.' "

19 Jacob ordered the second servant, the third servant and all the other servants to do the same thing.

Jacob thought,

"If I send this gift ahead of me, maybe Esau will forgive me. Then when I see him, perhaps he will accept me."

He said,

"Say the same thing to Esau when you meet him. 20 Say, 'Your servant Jacob is coming behind us.' "

21 So Jacob sent the gift to Esau. But Jacob stayed that night in the camp.

Jacob Wrestles with God

22 During the night Jacob rose and crossed the Jabbok River at the crossing. He took his 2 wives, his 2 slave girls and his 11 sons with him.

23 He sent his family and everything he had across the river.

24 But Jacob stayed behind alone. And a man came and wrestled with him until the sun came up. 25 The man saw that he could not defeat Jacob.

So he struck Jacob's hip and put it out of joint.

26 Then the man said to Jacob,

"Let me go. The sun is coming up."

But Jacob said,

"I will let you go if you will bless me."

27 The man said to him, "What is your name?" And he answered, "Jacob."

28 Then the man said, "Your name will no longer be Jacob. Your name will now be Israel," because you have wrestled with God and with men. And you have won."

29 Then Jacob asked him, "Please tell me your name." But the man said, "Why do you ask my name?"

Then he blessed Jacob there.

30 So Jacob named that place Peniel." He said, "I have seen God face to face. But my life was saved."

31 Then the sun rose as he was leaving that place. Jacob was limping because of his leg. 32 So even today the people of Israel do not eat the muscle that is on the hip joint of animals. This is because Jacob was touched there.

Chapter

33

Jacob Shows His Bravery

1 Jacob looked up and saw Esau coming. With him were 400 men. So Jacob divided his children among Leah, Rachel and the two slave girls.

2 Jacob put the slave girls with their children first. Then he put Leah and her children behind them. And he put Rachel and Joseph last.

32:28 Israel This name means "he wrestles with God."
32:30 Peniel This name means "the face of God."

91

3 Jacob himself went out in front of them. He bowed down flat on the ground seven times as he was walking toward his brother.

4 But Esau ran to meet Jacob.

Esau put his arms around him and hugged him. Then Esau kissed him, and they both cried.

5 Esau looked up and saw the women and children. He asked, "Who are these people with you?"

Jacob answered, "These are the children God has given me. God has been good to me, your servant."

6 Then the two slave girls and their children came up to Esau. They bowed down flat on the earth before him.

7 Then Leah and her children came up to Esau. They also bowed down flat on the earth. Last of all, Joseph and Rachel came up to Esau. And they, too, bowed down flat before him.

8 Esau said, "I saw many herds as I was coming here. Why did you bring them?"

Jacob answered, "They were to please you, my master."

9 But Esau said, "I already have enough, my brother. Keep what you have."

10 Jacob said,

"No! Please! If I have pleased you, then please accept the gift I give you. I am very happy to see your face again. It is like seeing the face of God because you have accepted me.

11 So I beg you to accept the gift I give you. God has been very good to me. And I have more than I need."

And because Jacob begged, Esau accepted the gift.

13 But Jacob said to him,

"My master, you know that the children are weak. And I must be careful with my flocks and their young ones. If I force them to go too far in one day, all the animals will die. 14 So, my master, you go on ahead of me, your servant. I will follow you slowly. I will let the animals and the children set the speed at which we travel. I will meet you, my master, in Edom."

12 Then Esau said,

"Let us get going. I will travel with you."

"No, thank you," said Jacob. "I only want to please you, my master."

15 So Esau said,

"Then let me leave some of my men with you."

16 So that day Esau started back to Edom. 17 But Jacob went to Succoth. There he built a house for himself. And he made shelters for his animals. That is why the place was named Succoth."

18 Jacob left Northwest Mesopotamia. And he arrived safely at the city of Shechem in the land of Canaan. He camped east of the city. 19 He bought a part of the field where he had camped. He bought it from the sons of Hamor father of Shechem for 100 pieces of silver.

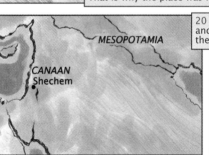

MESOPOTAMIA

CANAAN
Shechem

20 He built an altar there and named it after God, the God of Israel.

33:17 Succoth This name means "shelters."

93

Genesis 34:1-9

Chapter **34**

Dinah Is Attacked

1 Dinah was the daughter of Leah and Jacob. At this time Dinah went out to visit the women of that land.

2 Shechem son of Hamor the Hivite, the ruler of that land, saw Dinah.

He took her and forced her to have sexual relations with him.

3 Shechem fell in love with Dinah, and he spoke kindly to her.

4 He told his father, Hamor,

"Please get this girl for me so I can marry her."

5 Jacob learned how Shechem had disgraced his daughter. But Jacob's sons were out in the field with the cattle. So Jacob said nothing until they came home.

6 And Hamor father of Shechem went to talk with Jacob.

7 When Jacob's sons heard what had happened, they came in from the field. They were very angry, because Shechem had done such a wicked thing to Israel. It was wrong for him to have sexual relations with Jacob's daughter. A thing like this should not be done.

8 But Hamor talked to the brothers of Dinah. He said,

"My son Shechem is deeply in love with Dinah. Please let him marry her. 9 Marry our people. Give your women to our men as wives. And take our women for your men as wives.

10 "You can live in the same land with us. You will be free to own land and to trade here."

11 Shechem also talked to Jacob and to Dinah's brothers. He said,

"Please accept my offer. I will give anything you ask. 12 Ask as much as you want for the payment for the bride. I will give it to you. Just let me marry Dinah."

13 The sons of Jacob answered Shechem and his father with lies. They were angry because Shechem had disgraced their sister Dinah. 14 The brothers said to them,

"We cannot allow you to marry our sister. You are not circumcised.ᵈ That would be a disgrace to us. 15 But we will allow you to marry her if you do this one thing: Every man in your town must be circumcised like us. 16 Then your men can marry our women, and our men can marry your women. Then we will live in your land and become one people.

17 If you refuse to be circumcised, we will take Dinah and leave."

18 What they asked seemed fair to Hamor and Shechem. 19 So Shechem went quickly to be circumcised because he loved Jacob's daughter. Now Shechem was the most respected man in his family. 20 So Hamor and Shechem went to the gate of their city. They spoke to the men of their city. They said,

21 "These people want to be friends with us.

So let them live in our land and trade here. There is enough land for all of us. Let us marry their women. And we can let them marry our women. 22 But our men must agree to one thing. All our men must agree to be circumcised as they are. Then they will agree to live in our land. And we will be one people. 23 If we do this, their cattle and their animals will belong to us. Let us do what they say, and they will stay in our land."

95

Genesis 34:24-31

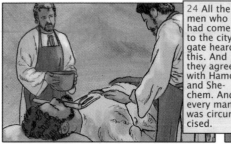

24 All the men who had come to the city gate heard this. And they agreed with Hamor and Shechem. And every man was circumcised.

25 Three days later the men who were circumcised were still in pain.

Two of Jacob's sons, Simeon and Levi (Dinah's brothers), took their swords. They made a surprise attack on the city. And they killed all the men there.

26 Simeon and Levi killed Hamor and his son Shechem.

Then they took Dinah out of Shechem's house and left.

27 Jacob's sons went among the dead bodies and stole everything that was in the city. This was to pay them back for what Shechem had done to their sister. 28 So the brothers took the flocks, herds and donkeys. And they took everything in the city and in the fields.

29 They took every valuable thing those people owned. They even took the wives and children and everything that was in the houses.

30 Then Jacob said to Simeon and Levi,

"You have caused me a lot of trouble. Now the Canaanites and the Perizzites who live in the land will hate me. There are only a few of us. If they join together to attack us, my people and I will be destroyed."

31 But the brothers said,

"We will not allow our sister to be treated like a prostitute."[d]

Chapter 35

Jacob in Bethel

1 God said to Jacob,

"Go to the city of Bethel and live there. Make an altar to the God who appeared to you there. This was when you were running away from your brother Esau."

2 So Jacob said to his family and to all who were with him,

"Put away the foreign gods you have. Make yourselves clean,[d] and change your clothes. 3 We will leave here and go to Bethel. There I will build an altar to God. He has helped me during my time of trouble. He has been with me everywhere I have gone."

4 So they gave Jacob all the foreign gods they had. And they gave him the earrings they were wearing.

He hid them under the great tree near the town of Shechem.

5 Then Jacob and his sons left there. But God caused the people in the nearby cities to be afraid. So they did not follow the sons of Jacob.

6 And Jacob and all the people who were with him went to Luz. It is now called Bethel. It is in the land of Canaan.

7 There Jacob built an altar. He named the place Bethel, after God, because God had appeared to him there. That was when he was running from his brother.

8 Deborah, Rebekah's nurse, died and was buried under the oak tree at Bethel. They named that place Oak of Crying.

Genesis 35:9-19

Jacob's New Name

9 When Jacob came back from Northwest Mesopotamia, God appeared to him again. And God blessed him. 10 God said to him,

"Your name is Jacob. But you will not be called Jacob any longer. Your new name will be Israel."

So he called him Israel. 11 God said to him,

"I am God All-Powerful. Have many children and grow in number as a nation. You will be the ancestor of many nations and kings. 12 I gave Abraham and Isaac land. I will give that same land to you and your descendants."[d]

13 Then God left him.

14 Jacob set up a stone on edge in that place where God had talked to him. And he poured a drink offering and olive oil on it to make it special for God. 15 And Jacob named the place Bethel.

Rachel Dies Giving Birth

16 Jacob and his group left Bethel. Before they came to Ephrath, Rachel began giving birth to her baby.

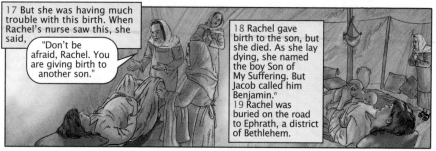

17 But she was having much trouble with this birth. When Rachel's nurse saw this, she said,

"Don't be afraid, Rachel. You are giving birth to another son."

18 Rachel gave birth to the son, but she died. As she lay dying, she named the boy Son of My Suffering. But Jacob called him Benjamin." 19 Rachel was buried on the road to Ephrath, a district of Bethlehem.

35:18 Benjamin This name means "right-hand son" or "favorite son."

20 And Jacob set up a rock on her grave to honor her. That rock is still there today.

21 Then Israel, also called Jacob, continued his journey. He camped just south of Migdal Eder.

22 While Israel was in that land Reuben had sexual relations with Israel's slave woman[d] Bilhah. And Israel heard about it.

The Family of Israel

Jacob had 12 sons. 23 He had 6 sons by his wife Leah. Reuben was his first son. Then Leah had Simeon, Levi, Judah, Issachar and Zebulun.
24 He had 2 sons by his wife Rachel: Joseph and Benjamin.
25 He had 2 sons by Rachel's slave girl Bilhah: Dan and Naphtali.
26 And he had 2 sons by Leah's slave girl Zilpah: Gad and Asher.
These are Jacob's sons who were born in Northwest Mesopotamia.
27 Jacob went to his father Isaac at Mamre near Hebron. This is where Abraham and Isaac had lived. 28 Isaac lived 180 years. 29 So Isaac breathed his last breath and died when he was very old. And his sons Esau and Jacob buried him.

Chapter 36

Esau's Family

1 This is the family history of Esau (also called Edom). 2 Esau married women from the land of Canaan. He married Adah daughter of Elon the Hittite. And he married Oholibamah daughter of Anah. Anah was the son of Zibeon the Hivite. And he married 3 Basemath, Ishmael's daughter, the sister of Nebaioth.
4 Adah gave Esau one son, Eliphaz. Basemath gave Esau Reuel. 5 And Oholibamah gave Esau Jeush, Jalam and Korah. These were Esau's sons who were born in the land of Canaan.
6 Esau took his wives, his sons, his daughters and all the people who lived with him. He took his herds and other animals. And he took all the belongings he had gotten in Canaan. And he went to a land away from his brother Jacob. 7 Esau and Jacob's belongings were becoming too many for them to live in the same land. The land where they had lived could not support both of them. They had too many herds. 8 So Esau lived in the mountains of Edom. (Esau is also named Edom.)

9 This is the family history of Esau. He is the ancestor of the Edomites, who live in the mountains of Edom.

10 Esau's sons were Eliphaz son of Adah and Esau, and Reuel son of Basemath and Esau.

11 Eliphaz had five sons: Teman, Omar, Zepho, Gatam and Kenaz. 12 Eliphaz also had a slave woman[d] named Timna. Timna and Eliphaz gave birth to Amalek. These were Esau's grandsons by his wife Adah.

13 Reuel had four sons: Nahath, Zerah, Shammah and Mizzah. These were Esau's grandsons by his wife Basemath.

14 Esau's third wife was Oholibamah. She was the daughter of Anah. (Anah was the son of Zibeon.) Esau and Oholibamah gave birth to Jeush, Jalam and Korah.

15 These were the leaders that came from Esau. Esau's first son was Eliphaz. From him came these leaders: Teman, Omar, Zepho, Kenaz, 16 Korah, Gatam and Amalek. These were the leaders that came from Eliphaz in the land of Edom. They were the grandsons of Adah.

17 Esau's son Reuel was the father of these leaders: Nahath, Zerah, Shammah and Mizzah. These were the leaders that came from Reuel in the land of Edom. They were the grandsons of Esau's wife Basemath.

18 Esau's wife Oholibamah gave birth to these leaders: Jeush, Jalam and Korah.

These are the leaders that came from Esau's wife Oholibamah. She was the daughter of Anah. 19 These were the sons of Esau (also called Edom), and these were their leaders.

20 These were the sons of Seir the Horite, who were living in the land: Lotan, Shobal, Zibeon, Anah, 21 Dishon, Ezer and Dishan. These sons of Seir were the leaders of the Horites in Edom.

22 The sons of Lotan were Hori and Homam. (Timna was Lotan's sister.)

23 The sons of Shobal were Alvan, Manahath, Ebal, Shepho and Onam.

24 The sons of Zibeon were Aiah and Anah. Anah is the man who found the hot springs in the desert. He found them while he was caring for his father's donkeys.

25 The children of Anah were Dishon and Oholibamah daughter of Anah.

26 The sons of Dishon were Hemdan, Eshban, Ithran and Keran.

27 The sons of Ezer were Bilhan, Zaavan and Akan.

28 The sons of Dishan were Uz and Aran.

29 These were the names of the Horite leaders: Lotan, Shobal, Zibeon, Anah, 30 Dishon, Ezer and Dishan. These men were the leaders of the Horite families. They lived in the land of Edom.

31 These are the kings who ruled in the land of Edom before the Israelites ever had a king.

32 Bela son of Beor was the king of Edom. He came from the city of Dinhabah.

33 When Bela died, Jobab son of Zerah became king. Jobab was from Bozrah.

34 When Jobab died, Husham became king. He was from the land of the Temanites.

35 When Husham died, Hadad son of Bedad became king. Hadad had defeated Midian in the country of Moab. Hadad was from the city of Avith.

36 When Hadad died, Samlah became king. He was from Masrekah.

37 When Samlah died, Shaul became king. He was from Rehoboth on the Euphrates River.

38 When Shaul died, Baal-Hanan son of Acbor became king.

39 When Baal-Hanan son of Acbor died, Hadad became king. He was from the city of Pau. His wife's name was Mehetabel daughter of Matred. Matred was the daughter of Me-Zahab.

40 These Edomite leaders came from Esau. They are listed by their families and regions. Their names were Timna, Alvah, Jetheth, 41 Oholibamah, Elah, Pinon, 42 Kenaz, Teman, Mibzar, 43 Magdiel and Iram. These were the leaders of Edom. (Esau was the father of the Edomites.) The area where each of these families lived was named after that family.

Chapter 37

Joseph the Dreamer

1 Jacob lived in the land of Canaan, where his father had lived. 2 This is the family history of Jacob. Joseph was a young man, 17 years old. He and his brothers cared for the flocks. His brothers were the sons of Bilhah and Zilpah, his father's wives.

Joseph gave his father bad reports about his brothers.

3 Joseph was born when his father Israel, also called Jacob, was old. So Israel loved Joseph more than his other sons. He made Joseph a special robe with long sleeves.

4 Joseph's brothers saw that their father loved Joseph more than he loved them. So they hated their brother and could not speak to him politely.

5 One time Joseph had a dream. When he told his brothers about it, they hated him even more.

6 Joseph said,

"Listen to the dream I had. 7 We were in the field tying bundles of wheat together. My bundle stood up, and your bundles of wheat gathered around mine. Your bundles bowed down to mine."

8 His brothers said,

"Do you really think you will be king over us? Do you truly think you will rule over us?"

His brothers hated him even more now. They hated him because of his dreams and what he had said.

9 Then Joseph had another dream. He told his brothers about it also. He said,

"Listen, I had another dream. I saw the sun, moon and 11 stars bowing down to me."

10 Joseph also told his father about this dream. But his father scolded him, saying,

"What kind of dream is this? Do you really believe that your mother, your brothers and I will bow down to you?"

11 Joseph's brothers were jealous of him. But his father thought about what all these things could mean.

12 One day Joseph's brothers went to Shechem to herd their father's sheep.

13 Jacob said to Joseph,

"Go to Shechem. Your brothers are there herding the sheep."

Joseph answered,

"I will go."

14 His father said,

"Go and see if your brothers and the sheep are all right. Then come back and tell me."

So Joseph's father sent him from the Valley of Hebron. When Joseph came to Shechem, 15 a man found him wandering in the field. He asked Joseph,

"What are you looking for?"

16 Joseph answered,

"I am looking for my brothers. Can you tell me where they are herding the sheep?"

17 The man said,

"They have already gone. I heard them say they were going to Dothan."

So Joseph went to look for his brothers and found them in Dothan.

Joseph Sold into Slavery

18 Joseph's brothers saw him coming from far away. Before he reached them, they made a plan to kill him.

19 They said to each other,

"Here comes that dreamer."

20 Let's kill him and throw his body into one of the wells. We can tell our father that a wild animal killed him. Then we will see what will become of his dreams."

21 But Reuben heard their plan and saved Joseph. He said,

Reuben planned to save Joseph later and send him back to his father.

23 So when Joseph came to his brothers, they pulled off his robe with long sleeves.

"Let's not kill him. 22 Don't spill any blood. Throw him into this well here in the desert. But don't hurt him!"

24 Then they threw him into the well. It was empty. There was no water in it.

25 While Joseph was in the well, the brothers sat down to eat.

When they looked up, they saw a group of Ishmaelites. They were traveling from Gilead to Egypt. Their camels were carrying spices, balm[d] and myrrh.[d]

Genesis 37:26-35

26 Then Judah said to his brothers,

"What will we gain if we kill our brother and hide his death? 27 Let's sell him to these Ishmaelites. Then we will not be guilty of killing our own brother. After all, he is our brother, our own flesh and blood."

And the other brothers agreed.

28 So when the Midianite traders came by, the brothers took Joseph out of the well. They sold him to the Ishmaelites for eight ounces of silver. And the Ishmaelites took him to Egypt.

29 Reuben was not with his brothers when they sold Joseph to the Ishmaelites. When Reuben came back to the well, Joseph was not there.

Reuben tore his clothes to show he was sad.

30 Then he went back to his brothers and said,

"The boy is not there! What will I do?"

31 The brothers killed a goat and dipped Joseph's long-sleeved robe in its blood.

32 Then they brought the robe to their father. They said,

"We found this robe. Look it over carefully. See if it is your son's robe."

33 Jacob looked it over and said,

"It is my son's robe! Some savage animal has eaten him. My son Joseph has been torn to pieces!"

34 Then Jacob tore his clothes and put on rough cloth to show that he was sad. He continued to be sad about his son for a long time. 35 All of Jacob's sons and daughters tried to comfort him.

104

But he could not be comforted. Jacob said,

"I will be sad about my son until the day I die."

So Jacob cried for his son Joseph.

36 Meanwhile the Midianites who had bought Joseph had taken him to Egypt. There they sold him to Potiphar. Potiphar was an officer to the king of Egypt and captain of the palace guard.

Chapter

38

Judah and Tamar

1 About that time, Judah left his brothers. He went to stay with a man named Hirah. Hirah was from the town of Adullam.

2 Judah met a Canaanite girl there and married her. Her father was named Shua.

And Judah had sexual relations with her. 3 She became pregnant and gave birth to a son. Judah named him Er. 4 Later she gave birth to another son. She named him Onan. 5 Later she had another son. She named him Shelah. She was at Kezib when this third son was born.

6 Judah chose a girl named Tamar to be the wife of his first son Er.

7 Er was Judah's oldest son. But he did what the Lord said was evil. So the Lord killed him. 8 Then Judah said to Er's brother Onan,

"Go and have sexual relations with your dead brother's wife." It is your duty to provide children for your brother in this way."

38:8 Go . . . wife. It was a custom in Israel that if a man died without children, one of his brothers would marry the widow. If a child was born, it would be considered the dead man's child.

Genesis 38:9-16

9 But Onan knew that the children would not belong to him. Onan was supposed to have sexual relations with Tamar. But he did not complete the sex act. This made it impossible for Tamar to become pregnant. So Er could not have descendants.[d]

11 Then Judah said to his daughter-in-law Tamar,

"Go back to live in your father's house. And don't marry until my young son Shelah grows up."

10 The Lord was displeased by this wicked thing Onan had done. So the Lord killed Onan also.

Judah was afraid that Shelah also would die like his brothers. So Tamar returned to her father's home.

12 After a long time Judah's wife, the daughter of Shua, died. After Judah had gotten over his sorrow, he went to Timnah. He went to his men who were cutting the wool from his sheep. His friend Hirah from Adullam went with him.

13 Tamar learned that Judah, her father-in-law, was going to Timnah to cut the wool from his sheep.

14 So she took off the clothes that showed she was a widow. Then she covered her face with a veil to hide who she was. She sat down by the gate of Enaim. It was on the road to Timnah. She did this because Judah's younger son Shelah had grown up. But Judah had not made plans for her to marry him.

15 When Judah saw her, he thought she was a prostitute.[d] This was because she had covered her face with a veil. 16 So Judah went to her and said,

"Let me have sexual relations with you."

He did not know that she was Tamar, his daughter-in-law. She asked,

"What will you give me if I let you have sexual relations with me?"

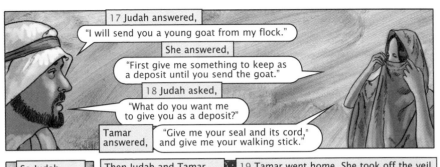

17 Judah answered,

"I will send you a young goat from my flock."

She answered,

"First give me something to keep as a deposit until you send the goat."

18 Judah asked,

"What do you want me to give you as a deposit?"

Tamar answered,

"Give me your seal and its cord, and give me your walking stick."

So Judah gave these things to her.

Then Judah and Tamar had sexual relations, and Tamar became pregnant.

19 Tamar went home. She took off the veil that covered her face. And she put on the clothes that showed she was a widow.

20 Judah sent his friend Hirah with the young goat. Judah told Hirah to find the woman and get back his seal and the walking stick he had given her. But Hirah could not find her. 21 Hirah asked some of the men at the town of Enaim,

"Where is the prostitute who was here by the road?"

The men answered,

"There has never been a prostitute here."

22 So he went back to Judah and said,

"I could not find the woman. The men who lived there said, 'There has never been a prostitute here.'"

23 Judah said,

"Let her keep the things. I don't want people to laugh at us. I sent her the goat as I promised. But you could not find her."

38:18 seal . . . cord A seal was used like a rubber stamp. People ran a string through it to tie around the neck. They wrote a contract, folded it, put wax or clay on the contract, and pressed the seal onto it as a signature.

Genesis 38:24-30

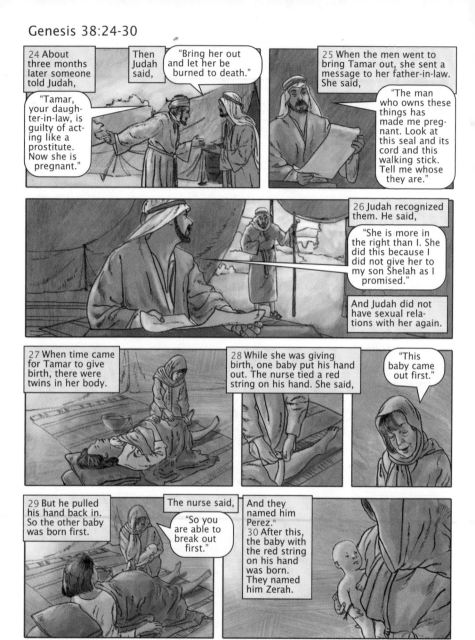

24 About three months later someone told Judah,

"Tamar, your daughter-in-law, is guilty of acting like a prostitute. Now she is pregnant."

Then Judah said,

"Bring her out and let her be burned to death."

25 When the men went to bring Tamar out, she sent a message to her father-in-law. She said,

"The man who owns these things has made me pregnant. Look at this seal and its cord and this walking stick. Tell me whose they are."

26 Judah recognized them. He said,

"She is more in the right than I. She did this because I did not give her to my son Shelah as I promised."

And Judah did not have sexual relations with her again.

27 When time came for Tamar to give birth, there were twins in her body.

28 While she was giving birth, one baby put his hand out. The nurse tied a red string on his hand. She said,

"This baby came out first."

29 But he pulled his hand back in. So the other baby was born first.

The nurse said,

"So you are able to break out first."

And they named him Perez.
30 After this, the baby with the red string on his hand was born. They named him Zerah.

38:29 Perez This name means "breaking out."

Chapter 39

Joseph Is Sold to Potiphar

1 Now Joseph had been taken down to Egypt. An Egyptian named Potiphar was an officer to the king of Egypt. He was the captain of the palace guard. He bought Joseph from the Ishmaelites who had brought him down there. 2 The Lord was with Joseph, and he became a successful man. He lived in the house of his master, Potiphar the Egyptian. 3 Potiphar saw that the Lord was with Joseph. He saw that the Lord made Joseph successful in everything he did. 4 So Potiphar was very happy with Joseph. He allowed Joseph to be his personal servant. He put Joseph in charge of the house. Joseph was trusted with everything Potiphar owned. 5 So Joseph was put in charge of the house. He was put in charge of everything Potiphar owned. Then the Lord blessed the people in Potiphar's house because of Joseph. And the Lord blessed everything that belonged to Potiphar, both in the house and in the field. 6 So Potiphar put Joseph in charge of everything he owned. Potiphar was not concerned about anything, except the food he ate.

Joseph Is Put into Prison

Now Joseph was well built and handsome. 7 After some time the wife of Joseph's master began to desire Joseph. One day she said to him,

"Have sexual relations with me."

8 But Joseph refused. He said to her,

"My master trusts me with everything in his house. He has put me in charge of everything he owns. 9 There is no one in his house greater than I. He has not kept anything from me, except you. And that is because you are his wife. How can I do such an evil thing? It is a sin against God."

10 The woman talked to Joseph every day, but he refused to have sexual relations with her or even spend time with her.

11 One day Joseph went into the house to do his work as usual. He was the only man in the house at that time. 12 His master's wife grabbed his coat. She said to him,

"Come and have sexual relations with me."

But Joseph left his coat in her hand and ran out of the house.

13 She saw what Joseph had done. He had left his coat in her hands and had run outside.

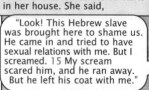

14 So she called to the servants in her house. She said,

"Look! This Hebrew slave was brought here to shame us. He came in and tried to have sexual relations with me. But I screamed. 15 My scream scared him, and he ran away. But he left his coat with me."

16 She kept his coat until her husband came home. 17 And she told her husband the same story. She said,

"This Hebrew slave you brought here came in to shame me! 18 When he came near me, I screamed. He ran away, but he left his coat."

19 When Joseph's master heard what his wife said Joseph had done, he became very angry.

20 So Potiphar arrested Joseph and put him into prison. This prison was where the king's prisoners were put.

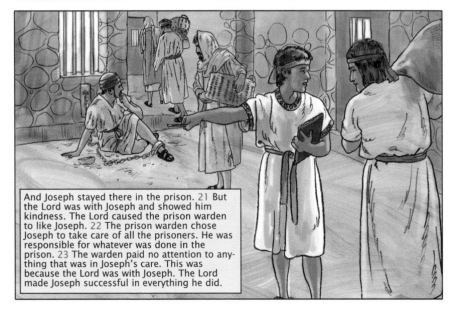

And Joseph stayed there in the prison. 21 But the Lord was with Joseph and showed him kindness. The Lord caused the prison warden to like Joseph. 22 The prison warden chose Joseph to take care of all the prisoners. He was responsible for whatever was done in the prison. 23 The warden paid no attention to anything that was in Joseph's care. This was because the Lord was with Joseph. The Lord made Joseph successful in everything he did.

Chapter

40

Joseph Interprets Two Dreams

1 After these things happened, two of the king's officers displeased the king. These officers were the man who served wine to the king and the king's baker. 2 The king became angry with his officer who served him wine and his baker. 3 So he put them in the prison of the captain of the guard. This was the same prison where Joseph was kept.

4 The captain of the guard put the two prisoners in Joseph's care. They stayed in prison for some time.

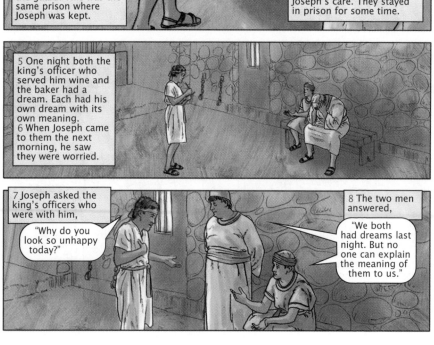

5 One night both the king's officer who served him wine and the baker had a dream. Each had his own dream with its own meaning. 6 When Joseph came to them the next morning, he saw they were worried.

7 Joseph asked the king's officers who were with him,

"Why do you look so unhappy today?"

8 The two men answered,

"We both had dreams last night. But no one can explain the meaning of them to us."

Joseph said to them,

"God is the only One who can explain the meaning of dreams. So tell me your dreams."

9 So the man who served wine to the king told Joseph his dream. He said,

"I dreamed I saw a vine. 10 On the vine there were three branches. I watched

the branches bud and blossom, and then the grapes ripened. 11 I was holding the king's cup.

So I took the grapes and squeezed the juice into the cup. Then I gave it to the king."

12 Then Joseph said,

"I will explain the dream to you. The three branches stand for three days. 13 Before the end of three days the king will free you. He will allow you to return to your work. You will serve the king his wine just as you did before.

Genesis 40:14-19

14 "But when you are free, remember me. Be kind to me. Tell the king about me so that I can get out of this prison.

15 I was taken by force from the land of the Hebrews. And I have done nothing here to deserve being put in prison."

16 The baker saw that Joseph's explanation of the dream was good. So he said to Joseph,

"I also had a dream. I dreamed there were three bread baskets on my head. 17 In the top basket there were all kinds of baked food for the king. But the birds were eating this food out of the basket on my head."

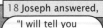

18 Joseph answered,

"I will tell you what the dream means. The three baskets stand for three days. 19 Before the end of three days, the king will cut off your head! He will hang your body on a pole. And the birds will eat your flesh."

20 Three days later it was the king's birthday. So he gave a feast for all his officers. In front of his officers, he let the chief officer who served his wine and the chief baker out of prison.

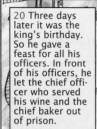

21 The king gave his chief officer who served wine his old position. Once again he put the king's cup of wine into the king's hand.

22 But the king hanged the baker on a pole. Everything happened just as Joseph had said it would. 23 But the officer who served wine did not remember Joseph. He forgot all about him.

Chapter 41

The King's Dreams

1 Two years later the king had a dream.

He dreamed he was standing on the bank of the Nile River. 2 He saw seven fat and beautiful cows come up out of the river. They stood there, eating the grass.

3 Then seven more cows came up out of the river. But they were thin and ugly. They stood beside the seven beautiful cows on the bank of the Nile.

4 The seven thin and ugly cows ate the seven beautiful fat cows. Then the king woke up.

5 The king slept again and dreamed a second time. In his dream he saw seven full and good heads of grain growing on one stalk. 6 After that, seven more heads of grain sprang up. But they were thin and burned by the hot east wind.

7 The thin heads of grain ate the seven full and good heads. Then the king woke up again. And he realized it was only a dream.

8 The next morning the king was troubled about these dreams. So he sent for all the magicians and wise men of Egypt.

The king told them his dreams. But no one could explain their meaning to him.

9 Then the chief officer who served wine to the king said to him,

"I remember something I promised to do. But I had forgotten about it. 10 There was a time when you were angry with me and the baker. You put us in prison in the house of the captain of the guard. 11 In prison we each had a dream on the same night. Each dream had a different meaning.

12 "A young Hebrew man was in the prison with us. He was a servant of the captain of the guard. We told him our dreams, and he explained their meanings to us. He told each man the meaning of his dream.

13 Things happened exactly as he said they would: I was given back my old position, and the baker was hanged."

14 So the king called for Joseph. The guards quickly brought him out of the prison. He shaved, put on clean clothes and went before the king. 15 The king said to Joseph,

"I have had a dream. But no one can explain its meaning to me. I have heard that you can explain a dream when someone tells it to you."

16 Joseph answered the king,

"I am not able to explain the meaning of dreams. God will do this for the king."

17 Then the king said to Joseph,

"In my dream I was standing on the bank of the Nile River. 18 I saw seven fat and beautiful cows. They came up out of the river and ate the grass. 19 Then I saw seven more cows come out of the river. They were thin and lean and ugly. They were the worst looking cows I have seen in all the land of Egypt. 20 And these thin and ugly cows ate the first seven fat cows. 21 But after they had eaten the seven cows, no one could tell they had eaten them. They just looked as thin and ugly as they did in the beginning. Then I woke up. 22 "I had another dream. I saw seven full and good heads of grain growing on one stalk. 23 Then seven more heads of grain sprang up after them. But these heads were thin and ugly. They were burned by the hot east wind.

24 "Then the thin heads ate the seven good heads. I told this dream to the magicians. But no one could explain its meaning to me."

Joseph Tells the Dreams' Meaning

25 Then Joseph said to the king,

"Both of these dreams mean the same thing. God is telling you what he is about to do.

26 The seven good cows stand for seven years. And the seven good heads of grain stand for seven years. Both dreams mean the same thing. 27 The seven thin and ugly cows stand for seven years. And the seven thin heads of grain burned by the hot east wind stand for seven years of hunger. 28 This will happen as I told you. God is showing the king what he is about to do. 29 You will have seven years of good crops and plenty to eat in all the land of Egypt. 30 But after those seven years, there will come seven years of hunger. All the food that grew in the land of Egypt will be forgotten. The time of hunger will eat up the land. 31 People will forget what it was like to have plenty of food. This is because the hunger that follows will be so great. 32 You had two dreams which mean the same thing. This shows that God has firmly decided that this will happen. And he will make it happen soon. 33 "So let the king choose a man who is very wise and understanding. Let the king set him over the land of Egypt. 34 And let the king also appoint officers over the land. They should take one-fifth of all the food that is grown during the seven good years. 35 They should gather all the food that is produced during the good years that are coming. Under the king's authority they should store the grain in the cities and guard it. 36 That food should be saved for later. It will be used during the seven years of hunger that will come on the land of Egypt. Then the people in Egypt will not die during the seven years of hunger."

Joseph Is Made Ruler over Egypt

37 This seemed like a very good idea to the king. All his officers agreed. 38 And the king asked them,

"Can we find a better man than Joseph to take this job? God's spirit is truly in him!"

39 So the king said to Joseph,

"God has shown you all this. There is no one as wise and understanding as you are.

40 I will put you in charge of my palace. All the people will obey your orders. Only I will be greater than you."

41 Then the king said to Joseph,

"Look! I have put you in charge of all the land of Egypt."

42 Then the king took off from his own finger his ring with the royal seal on it. And he put it on Joseph's finger.

He gave Joseph fine linen clothes to wear. And he put a gold chain around Joseph's neck.

43 The king had Joseph ride in the second royal chariot. Men walked ahead of his chariot calling,

"Bow down!"

By doing these things, the king put Joseph in charge of all of Egypt.

Genesis 41:44-52

44 The king said to him,

"I am the king. And I say that no one in all the land of Egypt may lift a hand or a foot unless you say he may."

45 The king gave Joseph the name Zaphenath-Paneah. He also gave Joseph a wife named Asenath. She was the daughter of Potiphera, priest of On. So Joseph traveled through all the land of Egypt.

46 Joseph was 30 years old when he began serving the king of Egypt. And he left the king's court and traveled through all the land of Egypt. 47 During the seven good years, the crops in the land grew well. 48 And Joseph gathered all the food produced in Egypt during those seven years of good crops. He stored the food in the cities. In every city he stored grain that had been grown in the fields around that city. 49 Joseph stored much grain, as much as the sand of the seashore. He stored so much grain that he could not measure it.

50 Joseph's wife was Asenath daughter of Potiphera, the priest of On. Before the years of hunger came, Joseph and Asenath had two sons. 51 Joseph named the first son Manasseh.[n] Joseph said,

"God has made me forget all the troubles I have had and all my father's family."

52 Joseph named the second son Ephraim.[n] Joseph said,

"God has given me children in the land of my troubles."

41:51 Manasseh This name sounds like the Hebrew word for "made me forget."
41:52 Ephraim This name sounds like the Hebrew word for "given me children."

53 The seven years of good crops came to an end in the land of Egypt. 54 Then the seven years of hunger began, just as Joseph had said. In all the lands people had nothing to eat. But in Egypt there was food. 55 The time of hunger became terrible in all of Egypt. The people cried to the king for food. He said to all the Egyptians,

"Go to Joseph. Do whatever he tells you to do."

56 The hunger was everywhere in that part of the world. And Joseph opened the storehouses and sold grain to the people of Egypt. This was because the time of hunger became terrible in Egypt. 57 And all the people in that part of the world came to Joseph in Egypt to buy grain. This was because the hunger was terrible everywhere in that part of the world.

Genesis 42:1-7

Chapter 42

The Dreams Come True

1 Jacob learned that there was grain in Egypt. So he said to his sons,

"Why are you just sitting here looking at one another? 2 I have heard that there is grain in Egypt. Go down there and buy grain for us to eat. Then we will live and not die."

3 So ten of Joseph's brothers went down to buy grain from Egypt. 4 But Jacob did not send Benjamin, Joseph's brother, with them.

Jacob was afraid that something terrible might happen to Benjamin.

5 Along with many other people, the sons of Jacob, also called Israel, went to Egypt to buy grain. This was because the people in the land of Canaan were hungry also. 6 Now Joseph was governor over Egypt. He was the one who sold the grain to people who came to buy it. So Joseph's brothers came to him. They bowed facedown on the ground before him.

7 When Joseph saw his brothers, he knew who they were. But he acted as if he didn't know them. He asked unkindly,

"Where do you come from?"

They answered,

"We have come from the land of Canaan to buy food."

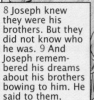

8 Joseph knew they were his brothers. But they did not know who he was. 9 And Joseph remembered his dreams about his brothers bowing to him. He said to them,

"You are spies! You came to learn where the nation is weak!"

10 But his brothers said to him,

"No, my master. We come as your servants just to buy food. 11 We are all sons of the same father. We are honest men, not spies."

12 Then Joseph said to them,

"No! You have come to learn where this nation is weak!"

13 And they said,

"We are 10 of 12 brothers. We are sons of the same father. We live in the land of Canaan. Our youngest brother is there with our father right now. And our other brother is gone."

14 But Joseph said to them,

"I can see I was right! You are spies! 15 But I will give you a way to prove you are telling the truth. As surely as the king lives, you will not leave this place until your youngest brother comes here.

16 One of you must go and get your brother. The rest of you will stay here in prison. We will see if you are telling the truth. If not, as surely as the king lives, you are spies."

17 Then Joseph put them all in prison for three days.

18 On the third day Joseph said to them,

"I am a God-fearing man. Do this thing, and I will let you live: 19 If you are honest men, let one of your brothers stay here in prison. The rest of you go and carry grain back to feed your hungry families. 20 Then bring your youngest brother back here to me. If you do this, I will know you are telling the truth. Then you will not die."

The brothers agreed to this.

123

Genesis 42:21-27

21 They said to each other,

"We are being punished for what we did to our brother. We saw his trouble. He begged us to save him, but we refused to listen. That is why we are in this trouble now."

22 Then Reuben said to them,

"I told you not to harm the boy. But you refused to listen to me. So now we are being punished for what we did to him."

23 When Joseph talked to his brothers, he used an interpreter. So they did not know that Joseph understood what they were saying. 24 Then Joseph left them and cried.

After a short time he went back and spoke to them. He took Simeon and tied him up while the other brothers watched.

25 Joseph told his servants to fill his brothers' bags with grain. They were to put the money the brothers had paid for the grain back in their bags. They were to give them things they would need for their trip back home. And the servants did this.

26 So the brothers put the grain on their donkeys and left.

27 When they stopped for the night, one of the brothers opened his sack. He was going to get food for his donkey.

Then he saw his money in the top of the sack.

124

28 He said to the other brothers,

"The money I paid for the grain has been put back. Here it is in my sack!"

The brothers were very frightened. They said to each other,

"What has God done to us?"

The Brothers Return to Jacob

29 The brothers went to their father Jacob in the land of Canaan. They told him everything that had happened. 30 They said,

"The master of that land spoke unkindly to us. He accused us of spying on his country. 31 But we told him that we were honest men, not spies.

32 We told him that we were 10 of 12 brothers—sons of one father. We said that 1 of our brothers was gone. And we said that our youngest brother was with our father in Canaan.
33 "Then the master of the land said to us, 'Here is a way I can know you are honest men: Leave 1 of your brothers with me. Take back grain to feed your hungry families, and go. 34 And bring your youngest brother to me. Then I will know that you are not spies but honest men. And I will give you back your brother whom you leave with me. And you can move about freely in our land.' "

35 Then the brothers emptied their sacks. And each of them found his money in his sack. When they and their father saw it, they were afraid.

Genesis 42:36–43:4

36 Their father Jacob said to them,

"You are robbing me of all my children. Joseph is gone. Simeon is gone. And now you want to take Benjamin away, too. Everything is against me."

37 Then Reuben said to his father,

"You may put my 2 sons to death if I don't bring Benjamin back to you. Trust him to my care. I will bring him back to you."

38 But Jacob said,

"I will not allow Benjamin to go with you. His brother is dead. He is the only son left from my wife Rachel. I am afraid something terrible might happen to him during the trip to Egypt. Then I would be sad until the day I die."

chapter 43

The Brothers Go Back to Egypt

1 Still no food grew in the land of Canaan. 2 Jacob's family had eaten all the grain they had brought from Egypt. So Jacob said to them,

"Go to Egypt again. Buy a little more grain for us to eat."

3 But Judah said to Jacob,

"The governor of that country strongly warned us. He said, 'Bring your brother back with you. If you don't, you will not be allowed to see me.' 4 If you will send Benjamin with us, we will go down and buy food for you.

5 "But if you refuse to send Benjamin, we will not go. The governor of that country warned us. He said we would not see him if we didn't bring Benjamin with us."

6 Jacob, also called Israel, said,

"Why did you tell the man you had another brother? You have caused me a lot of trouble."

7 The brothers answered,

"He questioned us carefully about ourselves and our family. He asked us, 'Is your father still alive? Do you have another brother?' We just answered his questions. How could we know he would ask us to bring our other brother to him?"

8 Then Judah said to his father Jacob,

"Send Benjamin with me. Then we will go at once. Do this so that we, you and our children may live and not die.

9 I will guarantee you that he will be safe. I will be personally responsible for him. If I don't bring him back to you, you can blame me all my life.

10 If we had not wasted all this time, we could have already made two trips."

11 Then their father Jacob said to them,

"If it has to be that way, then do this: Take some of the best foods in our land in your packs. Give them to the man as a gift: some balm,ᵈ some honey, spices, myrrh,ᵈ pistachio nuts and almonds.

12 Take twice as much money with you this time. Take back the money that was returned to you in your sacks last time. Maybe it was a mistake.

127

Genesis 43:13-18

13 "And take Benjamin with you. Now leave and go to the man. 14 I pray that God All-Powerful will cause the governor to be merciful to you. I pray that he will allow Simeon and Benjamin to come back with you. If I am robbed of my children, then I am robbed of them!"

15 So the brothers took the gifts. They also took twice as much money as they had taken the first time. And they took Benjamin.

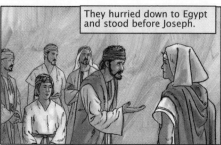

They hurried down to Egypt and stood before Joseph.

16 In Egypt Joseph saw Benjamin with them. Joseph said to the servant in charge of his house,

"Bring those men into my house. Kill an animal and prepare a meal. Those men will eat with me today at noon."

17 The servant did as Joseph told him. He brought the men to Joseph's house.

18 The brothers were afraid when they were brought to Joseph's house. They thought,

"We were brought here because of the money that was put in our sacks on the first trip. He wants to attack us, make us slaves and take our donkeys."

19 So the brothers went to the servant in charge of Joseph's house. They spoke to him at the door of the house. 20 They said,

"Sir, we came here once before to buy food. 21 While we were going home, we stopped for the night and opened our sacks. Each of us found all his money in his sack. We brought that money with us to give it back to you.

22 And we have brought more money. It is to pay for the food we want to buy this time. We don't know who put that money in our sacks."

23 But the servant answered,

"It's all right. Don't be afraid. Your God, the God of your father, must have put the money in your sacks. I got the money you paid me for the grain last time."

Then the servant brought Simeon out to them.

24 The servant led the men into Joseph's house. He gave them water, and they washed their feet. Then he gave their donkeys food to eat. 25 The men prepared their gift to give to Joseph when he arrived at noon. They had heard they were going to eat with him there.

26 When Joseph came home, the brothers gave him the gift they had brought into the house. Then they bowed down to the ground to him. 27 Joseph asked them how they were doing. He said,

"How is your aged father you told me about? Is he still alive?"

129

Genesis 43:28-34

28 The brothers answered,

"Your servant, our father, is well. He is still alive."

And they bowed low before Joseph to show him respect.

29 Then Joseph saw his brother Benjamin, who had the same mother as he. Joseph asked,

"Is this your youngest brother you told me about?"

Then Joseph said to Benjamin,

"God be good to you, my son!"

30 Then Joseph hurried off. He had to hold back the tears when he saw his brother Benjamin. So Joseph went into his room and cried there.

31 Then he washed his face and came out. He controlled himself and said,

"Serve the meal."

32 So they served Joseph at one table. They served his brothers at another table. And they served the Egyptians who ate with him at another table. This was because Egyptians did not like Hebrews and never ate with them. 33 Joseph's brothers were seated in front of him. They were in order of their ages, from oldest to youngest. And they looked at each other because they were so amazed. 34 Food from Joseph's table was taken to them. But Benjamin was given five times more food than the others. Joseph's brothers drank with him until they were very drunk.

Chapter

44

Joseph Sets a Trap

1 Then Joseph gave a command to the servant in charge of his house. Joseph said,

"Fill the men's sacks with as much grain as they can carry. And put each man's money into his sack with the grain. 2 Put my silver cup in the sack of the youngest brother. Also put his money for the grain in that sack."

The servant did what Joseph told him.

3 At dawn the brothers were sent away with their donkeys. 4 They were not far from the city when Joseph said to the servant in charge of his house,

"Go after the men. When you catch up with them, say, 'Why have you paid back evil for good? 5 The cup you have stolen is the one my master uses for drinking. And he uses it for explaining dreams. You have done a very wicked thing!'"

6 So the servant caught up with the brothers. He said to them what Joseph had told him to say. 7 But the brothers said to the servant,

"Why do you say these things? We would not do anything like that!

8 We brought back to you the money we found in our sacks. We brought it back from the land of Canaan. So surely we would not steal silver or gold from your master's house. 9 If you find that silver cup in the sack of one of us, then let him die. And we will be your slaves."

10 The servant said,

"We will do as you say. But only the man who has taken the cup will become my slave. The rest of you may go free."

11 Then every brother quickly lowered his sack to the ground and opened it. 12 The servant searched the sacks, going from the oldest brother to the youngest.

He found the cup in Benjamin's sack.

13 The brothers tore their clothes to show they were sad. Then they put their sacks back on the donkeys. And they returned to the city.

14 When Judah and his brothers went back to Joseph's house, Joseph was still there. The brothers bowed facedown on the ground before him.

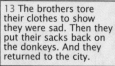

15 Joseph said to them,

"What have you done? Didn't you know that a man like me can learn things by signs and dreams?"

16 Judah said,

"Sir, what can we say? And how can we show we are not guilty?"

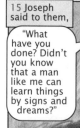

17 But Joseph said,

"I will not make you all slaves! Only the man who stole the cup will be my slave. The rest of you may go back safely to your father."

God has uncovered our guilt. So all of us will be your slaves, not just Benjamin."

18 Then Judah went to Joseph and said,

"Sir, please let me speak plainly to you. Please don't be angry with me. I know that you are as powerful as the king of Egypt himself. 19 When we were here before, you asked us, 'Do you have a father or a brother?' 20 And we answered you, 'We have an old father. And we have a younger brother. He was born when our father was old. This youngest son's brother is dead. So he is the only one of his mother's children left alive. And our father loves him very much.' 21 Then you said to us, 'Bring that brother to me. I want to see him.' 22 And we said to you, 'That young boy cannot leave his father. If he leaves him, his father would die.' 23 But you said to us, 'You must bring your youngest brother. If you don't, you will not be allowed to see me again.' 24 So we went back to our father and told him what you had said. 25 "Later, our father said, 'Go again. Buy us a little more food.' 26 We said to our father, 'We cannot go without our youngest brother. Without our youngest brother, we will not be allowed to see the governor.' 27 Then my father said to us, 'You know that my wife Rachel gave me two sons. 28 One son left me. I thought, "Surely he has been torn apart by a wild animal." And I haven't seen him since. 29 Now you want to take this son away from me also. But something terrible might happen to him. Then I would be sad until the day I die.' 30 Now what will happen if we go home to our father without our youngest brother? He is the most important thing in our father's life. 31 When our father sees that the young boy is not with us, he will die. And it will be our fault. We will cause the great sorrow that kills our father. 32 "I gave my father a guarantee that the young boy would be safe. I said to my father, 'If I don't bring him back to you, you can blame me all my life.' 33 So now, please allow me to stay here and be your slave. And let the young boy go back home with his brothers. 34 I cannot go back to my father if the boy is not with me. I couldn't stand to see my father that sad."

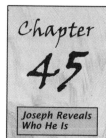

Chapter 45

Joseph Reveals Who He Is

1 Joseph could not control himself in front of his servants any longer. He cried out,

"Have everyone leave me."

When only the brothers were left with Joseph, he told them who he was.

2 Joseph cried so loudly that the Egyptians heard him. And the people in the king's palace heard about it.

3 He said to his brothers,

"I am Joseph. Is my father still alive?"

But the brothers could not answer him, because they were very afraid of him.

4 So Joseph said to them,

"Come close to me."

So the brothers came close to him. And he said to them,

"I am your brother Joseph. You sold me as a slave to go to Egypt.

5 Now don't be worried. Don't be angry with yourselves because you sold me here. God sent me here ahead of you to save people's lives."

6 "No food has grown on the land for two years now. And there will be five more years without planting or harvest. 7 So God sent me here ahead of you. This was to make sure you have some descendants[d] left on earth. And it was to keep you alive in an amazing way. 8 So it was not you who sent me here, but God. God has made me the highest officer of the king of Egypt. I am in charge of his palace. I am the master of all the land of Egypt. 9 "So leave quickly and go to my father. Tell him, 'Your son Joseph says: God has made me master over all Egypt. Come down to me quickly. 10 Live in the land of Goshen. You will be near me. Also your children, your grandchildren, your flocks and herds and all that you have will be near me. 11 I will care for you during the next five years of hunger. In this way, you and your family and all that you have will not starve.'

12 "Now you can see for yourselves. The one speaking to you is really Joseph. And my brother Benjamin can see this. 13 So tell my father about how powerful I have become in Egypt. Tell him about everything you have seen. Now hurry and bring him back to me."

14 Then Joseph hugged his brother Benjamin and cried. And Benjamin cried also.

15 Then Joseph kissed all his brothers. He cried as he hugged them. After this, his brothers talked with him.

16 The king of Egypt and his officers learned that Joseph's brothers had come. And they were very happy about this. 17 So the king said to Joseph, "Tell your brothers to load their animals and go back to the land of Canaan. 18 Tell them to bring their father and their families back here to me. I will give them the best land in Egypt. And they will eat the best food we have here. 19 Tell them to take some wagons from Egypt for their children and their wives. And tell them to bring their father back also. 20 Tell them not to worry about bringing any of their things with them. We will give them the best of what we have in Egypt."

21 So the sons of Israel did this. Joseph gave them wagons as the king had ordered. And he gave them food for their trip. 22 He gave each brother a change of clothes. But he gave Benjamin five changes of clothes. And Joseph gave him about seven and one-half pounds of silver.

23 Joseph also sent his father ten donkeys loaded with the best things from Egypt. And he sent ten female donkeys. They were loaded with grain, bread and other food for his father on his trip back. 24 Then Joseph told his brothers to go. As they were leaving, he said to them,

"Don't quarrel on the way home."

25 So the brothers left Egypt and went to their father Jacob in the land of Canaan. 26 They told him,

"Joseph is still alive. He is the ruler over all the land of Egypt."

Their father was shocked and did not believe them.

27 But the brothers told him everything Joseph had said. Then Jacob saw the wagons that Joseph had sent to carry him back to Egypt. Now Jacob felt better. 28 Jacob, also called Israel, said,

"Now I believe you. My son Joseph is still alive. I will go and see him before I die."

Chapter 46

Jacob Goes to Egypt

1 So Jacob, also called Israel, took all he had and started his trip. He went to Beersheba. There he offered sacrifices to the God of his father Isaac.

2 During the night God spoke to Israel in a vision. He said,

"Jacob, Jacob."

And Jacob answered,

"Here I am."

3 Then God said,

"I am God, the God of your father. Don't be afraid to go to Egypt. I will make your descendants[d] a great nation there. 4 I will go to Egypt with you. And I will bring you out of Egypt again. Joseph's own hands will close your eyes when you die."

Genesis 46:5-27

5 Then Jacob left Beersheba. The sons of Israel loaded their father, their children and their wives. They put them in the wagons the king of Egypt had sent. 6 They also took their farm animals and everything they had gotten in Canaan. So Jacob went to Egypt with all his descendants. 7 He took his sons and grandsons, his daughters and granddaughters. He took all his family to Egypt with him.

Jacob's Family

8 Now these are the names of the children of Israel who went into Egypt. (They are Jacob and his descendants.^d) Reuben was Jacob's first son. 9 Reuben's sons were Hanoch, Pallu, Hezron and Carmi. 10 Simeon's sons were Jemuel, Jamin, Ohad, Jakin, Zohar and Shaul. (Shaul was Simeon's son by a Canaanite woman.) 11 Levi's sons were Gershon, Kohath and Merari. 12 Judah's sons were Er, Onan, Shelah, Perez and Zerah. (But Er and Onan had died in the land of Canaan.) Perez's sons were Hezron and Hamul. 13 Issachar's sons were Tola, Puah, Jashub and Shimron. 14 Zebulun's sons were Sered, Elon and Jahleel. 15 These are the sons of Leah and Jacob born in Northwest Mesopotamia. His daughter Dinah was also born there. There were 33 persons in this part of Jacob's family. 16 Gad's sons were Zephon, Haggi, Shuni, Ezbon, Eri, Arodi and Areli. 17 Asher's sons were Imnah, Ishvah, Ishvi and Beriah. Their sister was Serah. Beriah's sons were Heber and Malkiel. 18 These are Jacob's sons by Zilpah. She was the slave girl whom Laban gave to his daughter Leah. There were 16 persons in this part of Jacob's family.

19 The sons of Jacob's wife Rachel were Joseph and Benjamin. 20 In Egypt, Joseph became the father of Manasseh and Ephraim by his wife Asenath. She was the daughter of Potiphera, priest of On. 21 Benjamin's sons were Bela, Beker, Ashbel, Gera, Naaman, Ehi, Rosh, Muppim, Huppim and Ard. 22 These are the sons of Jacob by his wife Rachel. There were 14 persons in this part of Jacob's family. 23 Dan's son was Hushim. 24 Naphtali's sons were Jahziel, Guni, Jezer and Shillem. 25 These are Jacob's sons by Bilhah. She was the slave girl whom Laban gave to his daughter Rachel. There were 7 persons in this part of Jacob's family. 26 So the total number of Jacob's direct descendants who went to Egypt was 66. (The wives of Jacob's sons were not counted in this number.) 27 Joseph had 2 sons born in Egypt. So the total number in the family of Jacob in Egypt was 70.

138

Jacob Arrives in Egypt

28 Jacob sent Judah ahead of him to see Joseph in Goshen. Then Jacob and his people came into the land of Goshen. 29 Joseph prepared his chariot and went to meet his father Israel in Goshen.

As soon as Joseph saw his father, he hugged his neck. And he cried there for a long time.

30 Then Israel said to Joseph,

"Now I am ready to die. I have seen your face. And I know that you are still alive."

31 Joseph said to his brothers and his father's family,

"I will go and tell the king you are here. I will say, 'My brothers and my father's family have left the land of Canaan. They have come here to me. 32 They are shepherds and take care of farm animals. And they have brought their flocks and their herds and everything they own with them.' 33 When the king calls you, he will ask, 'What work do you do?' 34 This is what you should tell him: 'We, your servants, have taken care of farm animals all our lives. Our ancestors did the same thing.' Then the king will allow you to settle in the land of Goshen. This is away from the Egyptians. They don't like to be near shepherds."

Chapter

47

*Jacob Settles
in Goshen*

1 Joseph went in to the king and said,

"My father and my brothers have arrived from Canaan. They have their flocks and herds and everything they own with them. They are now in the land of Goshen."

2 Joseph chose five of his brothers to introduce to the king. 3 The king said to the brothers,

"What work do you do?"

And they said to him,

"We, your servants, are shepherds. Our ancestors were also shepherds."

4 They said to the king,

"We have come to live in this land. There is no grass in the land of Canaan for our animals to eat. The hunger is very terrible there.

So please allow us to live in the land of Goshen."

5 Then the king said to Joseph,

"Your father and your brothers have come to you. 6 You may choose any place in Egypt for them to live. Give your father and your brothers the best land. Let them live in the land of Goshen. And if any of them are skilled shepherds, put them in charge of my sheep and cattle."

7 Then Joseph brought in his father Jacob and introduced him to the king. And Jacob blessed the king. 8 Then the king said to Jacob,

"How old are you?"

9 Jacob said to him,

"My life has been spent wandering from place to place. It has been short, filled with trouble. I have lived only 130 years. My ancestors lived much longer than I."

10 Then Jacob blessed the king and left.

11 Joseph obeyed the king. He gave his father and brothers the best land in Egypt. It was near the city of Rameses. 12 And Joseph gave his father, his brothers and everyone who lived with them the food they needed.

Joseph Buys Land for the King

13 The hunger became worse, and there was no food anywhere in the land. The land of Egypt and the land of Canaan became very poor because of this. 14 Joseph collected all the money that was to be found in Egypt and Canaan. People paid him this money for the grain they were buying. He brought that money to the king's palace.

15 After some time, the people in Egypt and Canaan had no money left. So they went to Joseph and said,

"Please give us food. Our money is gone. If we don't eat, we will die here in front of you."

16 Joseph answered,

"Since you have no money, give me your farm animals. I will give you food in return."

17 So people brought their farm animals to Joseph. And he gave them food in exchange for their horses, sheep, cattle and donkeys. So he kept them alive by trading food for their farm animals that year.

Genesis 47:18-26

18 The next year the people came to Joseph and said,

"You know we have no money left. And all our animals belong to you. We have nothing left except our bodies and our land.

19 Surely both we and our land will die here in front of you. Buy us and our land in exchange for food. And we will be slaves to the king, together with our land. Give us seed to plant. Then we will live and not die. And the land will not become a desert."

20 So Joseph bought all the land in Egypt for the king. Every Egyptian sold Joseph his field, because the hunger was very great. So the land became the king's.

21 And Joseph made the people slaves from one end of Egypt to the other.

22 The only land he did not buy was the land the priests owned. They did not need to sell their land because the king paid them for their work. So they had money to buy food.

23 Joseph said to the people,

"Now I have bought you and your land for the king. So I will give you seed. And you can plant your fields. **24** At harvest time you must give one-fifth to the king. You may keep four-fifths for yourselves. Use it as seed for the field and as food for yourselves, your families and your children."

25 The people said,

"You have saved our lives. If you like, we will become slaves of the king."

26 So Joseph made a law in Egypt, which continues today: One-fifth of everything from the land belongs to the king. The only land the king did not get was the priests' land.

"Don't Bury Me in Egypt"

27 The Israelites continued to live in the land of Goshen in Egypt. There they got possessions. They had many children and grew in number.

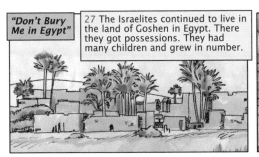

28 Jacob, also called Israel, lived in Egypt 17 years. So he lived to be 147 years old.

29 Israel knew he soon would die. So he called his son Joseph to him. He said to Joseph,

"If you love me, put your hand under my leg.[n] Promise me you will not bury me in Egypt. 30 When I die, carry me out of Egypt. Bury me where my ancestors are buried."

Joseph answered,

"I will do as you say."

31 Then Jacob said,

"Promise me."

And Joseph promised him that he would do this. Then Israel worshiped as he leaned on the top of his walking stick.

Chapter 48

Blessings for Manasseh and Ephraim

1 Some time later Joseph learned that his father was very sick.

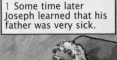

So he took his two sons Manasseh and Ephraim and went to his father. 2 When Joseph arrived, someone told Jacob, also called Israel,

"Your son Joseph has come to see you."

Jacob was weak. So he used all his strength and sat up on his bed.

47:29 put . . . leg This showed that a person would keep a promise.

Genesis 48:3-10

3 Then Jacob said to Joseph,

"God All-Powerful appeared to me at Luz in the land of Canaan. God blessed me there. 4 He said to me, 'I will give you many children. I will make you the father of many peoples. And I will give your descendants[d] this land forever.' 5 Your two sons were born here in Egypt before I came. They will be counted as my own sons. Ephraim and Manasseh will be my sons just as Reuben and Simeon are my sons. 6 But if you have other children, they will be your own. But their land will be part of the land given to Ephraim and Manasseh. 7 When I came from Northwest Mesopotamia, Rachel died in the land of Canaan. We were traveling toward Ephrath. This made me very sad. I buried her there beside the road to Ephrath." (Today Ephrath is Bethlehem.)

8 Then Israel saw Joseph's sons. He said,

"Who are these boys?"

9 Joseph said to his father,

"They are my sons. God has given them to me here in Egypt."

Israel said,

"Bring your sons to me so I may bless them."

10 At this time Israel's eyesight was bad because he was old. So Joseph brought the boys close to him. Israel kissed the boys and put his arms around them.

11 He said to Joseph,

"I thought I would never see you alive again. And now God has let me see you and also your children."

12 Then Joseph moved his sons off Israel's lap. Joseph bowed facedown to the ground.

13 He put Ephraim on his right side and Manasseh on his left. (So Ephraim was near Israel's left hand, and Manasseh was near Israel's right hand.) Joseph brought the boys close to Israel. 14 But Israel crossed his arms. He put his right hand on the head of Ephraim, who was younger. He put his left hand on the head of Manasseh. But he was the firstborn[d] son. 15 And Israel blessed Joseph and said,

"My ancestors Abraham and Isaac served our God. And like a shepherd God has led me all my life. 16 He was the Angel who saved me from all my troubles. Now I pray that he will bless these boys. May my name be known through these boys. And may the names of my ancestors Abraham and Isaac be known through them. May they have many descendants[d] on the earth."

17 Joseph saw that his father put his right hand on Ephraim's head. Joseph didn't like it. So he took hold of his father's hand. He wanted to move it from Ephraim's head to Manasseh's head. 18 Joseph said to his father,

"You are doing it wrong, Father. Manasseh is the firstborn son. Put your right hand on his head."

145

19 But his father refused and said,

"I know, my son, I know. Manasseh will be great and have many descendants. But his younger brother will be greater.

And his descendants will be enough to make a nation."

20 So Israel blessed them that day. He said,

"When a blessing is given in Israel, they will say: 'May God make you like Ephraim and Manasseh.'"

In this way he made Ephraim greater than Manasseh.

21 Then Israel said to Joseph,

"Look at me. I am about to die. But God will be with you. He will take you back to the land of your fathers.

22 I have given you something that I did not give your brothers. I have given you the land of Shechem that I took from the Amorite people. I took it with my sword and my bow."

Chapter

49

Jacob Blesses His Sons

1 Then Jacob called his sons to him. He said,

"Come here to me. I will tell you what will happen to you in the future.

2 "Come together and listen, sons of Jacob. Listen to Israel, your father."
3 "Reuben, my first son, you are my strength. Your birth showed I could be a father. You have the highest position among my sons. You are the most powerful. 4 But you are uncontrolled like water. So you will no longer lead your brothers. This is because you got into your father's bed. You shamed me by having sexual relations with my slave girl.
5 "Simeon and Levi are brothers. They used their swords to do violence. 6 I will not join their secret talks. I will not meet with them to plan evil. They killed men because they were angry. And they crippled oxen just for fun. 7 May their anger be cursed, because it is too violent. May their violence be cursed, because it is too cruel. I will divide them up among the tribes[d] of Jacob. I will scatter them through all the tribes of Israel.

8 "Judah, your brothers will praise you. You will grab your enemies by the neck. Your brothers will bow down to you. 9 Judah is like a young lion. You have returned from killing, my son. Like a lion, he stretches out and lies down to rest. No one is brave enough to wake him. 10 Men from Judah's family will be kings. Someone from Judah will always be on the throne. Judah will rule until the real king comes. And the nations will obey him. 11 He ties his donkey to a grapevine. He ties his young donkey to the best branch. He can afford to use wine to wash his clothes. He even uses grape juice to wash his robes. 12 His eyes are bright from drinking wine. His teeth are white from drinking milk.
13 "Zebulun will live near the sea. His shore will be a safe place for ships. His land will reach as far as Sidon.
14 "Issachar is like a strong donkey. He lies down while

carrying his load. 15 He will see his resting place is good. He will see how pleasant his land is. Then he will put his back to the load. He will become a slave.
16 "Dan will rule his own people like the other tribes in Israel. 17 Dan will be a snake by the side of the road. He will be like a dangerous snake lying near the path. That snake bites a horse's leg. And the rider is thrown off backward.
18 "Lord, I wait for your salvation.
19 "Robbers will attack Gad. But he will defeat them and drive them away.
20 "Asher's land will grow much good food. He will grow food fit for a king.
21 "Naphtali is like a female deer that runs free. She has beautiful fawns.
22 "Joseph is like a grapevine that produces much fruit. He is like a healthy vine watered by a spring. He is like a vine whose branches grow over the wall.

23 "Men attack him violently with arrows. They shoot at him angrily. 24 But he aims his bow well. His arms are made strong. He gets his power from the Mighty God of Jacob. He gets his strength from the Shepherd, the Rock[d] of Israel. 25 Your father's God helps you. God All-Powerful blesses you. He blesses you with rain from above. He blesses you with water from springs below. He blesses you with many babies born to your wives. He blesses you with many young ones born to your animals. 26 The blessings of your father are greater than the blessings of the oldest mountains. They are greater than the good things of the long-lasting hills. May these blessings rest on the head of Joseph. May they rest on the forehead of the one who was separated from his brothers. 27 "Benjamin is like a hungry wolf. In the morning he eats what he has caught. In the evening he divides what he has taken."

28 These are the 12 tribes of Israel. And this is what their father said to them. He gave each son the blessing that was right for him. 29 Then Israel gave them a command. He said,

"I am about to die. Bury me with my ancestors in the cave in the field of Ephron the Hittite. 30 That cave is in the field of Machpelah east of Mamre. It is in the land of Canaan. Abraham bought that field from Ephron the Hittite for a burying place. 31 Abraham and Sarah his wife are buried there. Isaac and Rebekah his wife are buried there. I buried my wife Leah there. 32 The field and the cave in it were bought from the Hittite people."

33 After Jacob finished talking to his sons, he lay down. He put his feet back on the bed, took his last breath and died.

Chapter

50

Jacob's
Burial

1 When Jacob died, Joseph hugged his father and cried over him and kissed him.

2 He commanded the doctors who served him to prepare his father's body. So the doctors prepared Jacob's body to be buried.

3 It took the doctors 40 days to prepare his body. This was the usual time it took. And the Egyptians had a time of sorrow for Jacob. It lasted 70 days.

4 When this time of sorrow had ended, Joseph spoke to the king's officers. He said,

"If you think well of me, please tell this to the king:

5 'When my father was near death, I made a promise to him. I promised I would bury him in a cave in the land of Canaan. This is a burial place that he cut out for himself. So please let me go and bury my father. Then I will return.' "

6 The king answered,

"Keep your promise. Go and bury your father."

7 So Joseph went to bury his father. All the king's officers, the elders of his court and all the elders of Egypt went with Joseph.

Genesis 50:8-13

8 Everyone who lived with Joseph and his brothers went with him. And everyone who lived with his father also went. They left only their children, their flocks and their herds in the land of Goshen. 9 Men in chariots and on horses also went with Joseph. It was a very large group.
10 They went to the threshingᵈ floor of Atad, east of the Jordan River. There they cried loudly and bitterly for Jacob, also called Israel. Joseph's time of sorrow continued for seven days.
11 The people that lived in Canaan saw the sadness at the threshing floor of Atad. They said,

"Those Egyptians are showing great sorrow!"

So now that place is named Sorrow of the Egyptians.

12 So Jacob's sons did what their father commanded. 13 They carried his body to the land of Canaan. They buried it in the cave in the field of Machpelah near Mamre. Abraham had bought this cave and field from Ephron the Hittite. He bought the cave to use as a burial place.

14 After Joseph buried his father, he returned to Egypt. His brothers and everyone who had gone with him to bury his father also returned.

The Brothers Fear Joseph

15 After Jacob died, Joseph's brothers said,

"What if Joseph is still angry with us? We did many wrong things to him. What if he plans to pay us back?"

16 So they sent a message to Joseph. It said,

"Your father gave this command before he died. 17 He said to us, 'You have done wrong. You have sinned and done evil to Joseph. Tell Joseph to forgive you, his brothers.' So now, Joseph, we beg you to forgive our wrong. We are the servants of the God of your father."

When Joseph received the message, he cried.

18 And his brothers went to him and bowed low before him. They said,

"We are your slaves."

19 Then Joseph said to them,

"Don't be afraid. Can I do what only God can do? 20 You meant to hurt me. But God turned your evil into good. It was to save the lives of many people. And it is being done. 21 So don't be afraid. I will take care of you and your children."

So Joseph comforted his brothers and spoke kind words to them.

Genesis 50:22-26

22 Joseph continued to live in Egypt with all his father's family. He died when he was 110 years old. 23 During Joseph's life Ephraim had children and grandchildren. And Joseph's son Manasseh had a son named Makir. Joseph accepted Makir's children as his own.

The Death of Joseph

24 Joseph said to his brothers,

"I am about to die. But God will take care of you. He will lead you out of this land. He will lead you to the land he promised to Abraham, Isaac and Jacob."

25 Then Joseph had the sons of Israel make a promise. He said,

"Promise me that you will carry my bones with you out of Egypt."

26 Joseph died when he was 110 years old. Doctors prepared his body for burial. Then they put him in a coffin in Egypt.